INSIGHT POCKET GUIDE

SCOTLAND

20

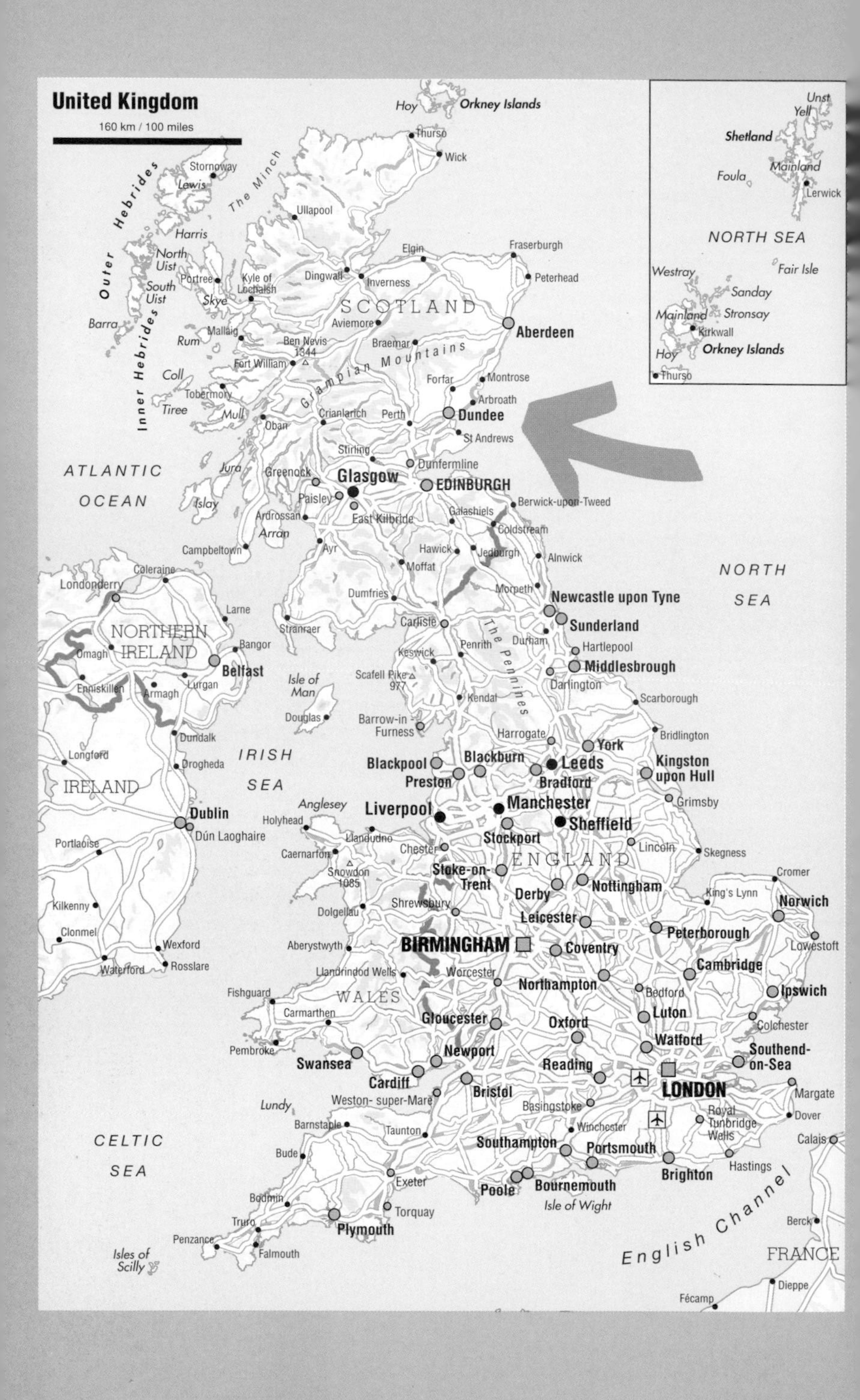

United Kingdom
160 km / 100 miles
Orkney Islands
Hoy
Thurso
Wick
Stornoway
Lewis
Outer Hebrides
The Minch
Ullapool
Harris
North Uist
South Uist
Barra
Portree
Kyle of Lochalsh
Skye
Dingwall
Inverness
Elgin
Fraserburgh
Peterhead
SCOTLAND
Aviemore
Aberdeen
Rum
Mallaig
Ben Nevis 1344
Braemar
Grampian Mountains
Fort William
Inner Hebrides
Coll
Tobermory
Tiree
Mull
Oban
Crianlarich
Perth
Forfar
Montrose
Arbroath
Dundee
St Andrews
Stirling
Dunfermline
Jura
Greenock
Glasgow
EDINBURGH
Islay
Paisley
East Kilbride
Ardrossan
Arran
Berwick-upon-Tweed
Galashiels
Coldstream
Campbeltown
Ayr
Hawick
Jedburgh
Moffat
Alnwick
ATLANTIC OCEAN
Coleraine
Londonderry
NORTHERN IRELAND
Larne
Omagh
Bangor
Belfast
Enniskillen
Armagh
Lurgan
Stranraer
Dumfries
Morpeth
Newcastle upon Tyne
Sunderland
Carlisle
The Pennines
Penrith
Durham
Hartlepool
Keswick
Middlesbrough
Darlington
Scafell Pike 977
Isle of Man
Douglas
Kendal
Scarborough
Barrow-in-Furness
Harrogate
Bridlington
York
Dundalk
Longford
Drogheda
IRISH SEA
Blackpool
Blackburn
Leeds
Preston
Bradford
Kingston upon Hull
IRELAND
Anglesey
Liverpool
Manchester
Grimsby
Dublin
Dún Laoghaire
Holyhead
Sheffield
Stockport
Llandudno
Lincoln
Skegness
Portlaoise
Caernarfon
Chester
Snowdon 1085
ENGLAND
Stoke-on-Trent
Derby
Nottingham
Cromer
King's Lynn
Norwich
Kilkenny
Dolgellau
Shrewsbury
Leicester
Clonmel
Peterborough
Lowestoft
Wexford
Aberystwyth
BIRMINGHAM
Coventry
Waterford
Rosslare
Llandrindod Wells
Worcester
Cambridge
Northampton
Ipswich
Fishguard
WALES
Bedford
Carmarthen
Gloucester
Luton
Colchester
Oxford
Pembroke
Newport
Watford
Southend-on-Sea
Swansea
Reading
Cardiff
Bristol
LONDON
Margate
Lundy
Weston-super-Mare
Basingstoke
Royal Tunbridge Wells
Dover
Barnstaple
Taunton
Winchester
CELTIC SEA
Southampton
Portsmouth
Calais
Bude
Brighton
Hastings
Exeter
Poole
Bournemouth
Bodmin
Isle of Wight
Torquay
Truro
Plymouth
Berck
Penzance
Falmouth
English Channel
FRANCE
Isles of Scilly
Dieppe
Fécamp
NORTH SEA
Unst
Yell
Shetland
Mainland
Foula
Lerwick
NORTH SEA
Fair Isle
Westray
Sanday
Mainland
Stronsay
Kirkwall
Hoy
Orkney Islands
Thurso

Welcome!

This guidebook combines the interests and enthusiasms of two of the world's best-known information providers: Insight Guides, who have set the standard for visual travel guides since 1970, and Discovery Channel, the world's premier source of non-fiction television programming.

Its aim is to help visitors get the most out of a short trip to this dramatic land. A series of itineraries help first-time visitors experience one of the wildest landscapes in Europe, as well as some of her most vibrant cities: elegant Edinburgh, dynamic Glasgow, historic St Andrews, and the capital of the Highlands, Inverness. Included are full-day tours of Edinburgh and Glasgow, a series of full-day and half-day drives to towns and sights close by, an excursion to the Borders, a visit to St Andrews and Fife, and a grand two-day tour of the Highlands, visiting Loch Lomond, the Isle of Skye, Loch Ness and Inverness. The itineraries are supported by imaginative suggestions on where to eat and where to stay along the way.

Marcus Brooke was born and educated in Scotland and, although he has lived and worked as a writer and photographer in far-flung parts of the world, he returns to his home patch frequently. He delights in the beauty of the Scottish landscape and seascape, although he does, at times, despair of the weather: 'A Scotsman can hold his drink but the clouds cannot hold theirs,' he says. But as he points out, it is because of the weather that Scotland is so green and lush and not overrun by tourists. And how, without the weather, would there be such superb fishing and such delectable whisky?

C O N T E N T S

History & Culture

Scotland's Highlights

The first two full-day itineraries focus on the highlights of Edinburgh and Glasgow, while the third provides a taste of the Highlands in a visit to Stirling and the Trossachs.

Pages 2/3: Quiet moment at Monteith

Pick & Mix Itineraries

These seven shorter itineraries concentrate on other interesting aspects and areas of Edinburgh, and towns within easy reach.

Excursions

For visitors with more time to spare, three longer excursions to the Border region, St Andrews and Fife and the Isle of Skye.

Shopping, Eating Out and Nightlife

Calendar of Special Events

Practical Information

Maps

Pages 8/9: the Military Tattoo at Edinburgh Castle

History &

The first Christian missionary to Scotland was St Ninian, who arrived about 400AD, followed in 563 by St Columba, who is said to have scared off the Loch Ness monster with the sign of the cross and an invocation. At that time Scotland was divided into four kingdoms, three of them inhabited by Celts – Picts, Scots and Britons. The fourth tribe was the Angles, a Teutonic people who had extended their rule into Lothian from Northumbria. Add to this the Norsemen who, in the 9th century, established themselves in the extreme north.

Warfare among all these groups was incessant, but careful diplomatic marriage resulted in some unity between the Picts and Scots under Kenneth MacAlpin, King of Scots. However, not until 1018, when his descendant Malcolm II defeated the Angles, did the Lothians come under Scottish rule. In that year the King of the Britons of

William Wallace rallies his men against the English

Culture

Strathclyde died and was succeeded by Malcolm's grandson, Duncan. Thus was born the Kingdom of Scotland, with Duncan I its king. (The Norsemen still held their own territory.)

Duncan was slain by Macbeth (as in the Shakespeare play of the same name) who, in turn, was killed by Duncan's elder son Malcolm III, who thus regained his father's throne. Malcolm's English upbringing and his English wife Margaret, a granddaughter of England's Edward the Confessor and a refugee after the Norman Conquest of England in 1066, were harbingers of English and Norman involvement in Scottish affairs.

Mary Queen of Scots

On the death in 1290 of the Maid of Norway, heir to the throne, England's Edward I declared himself feudal overlord and selected John Balliol as his vassal king. Foolishly, Balliol repudiated allegiance to Edward, concluded an alliance with France and in 1296 prepared to invade England. Thus began the Wars of Independence (1296–1330) in which Edward, Hammer of the Scots, attempted to dominate the Scots. The wars produced many Scottish heroes including William Wallace and Robert the Bruce. Success finally came to the latter against the ineffectual Edward II in 1314, a date no Scot ever forgets, with victory over the English at the Battle of Bannockburn. Recognition of Scotland as an independent kingdom came with the treaty of Northampton in 1328. Bruce's son David II was succeeded by Robert II, the first of the Stewarts (or French-style 'Stuarts').

Over the ensuing centuries an uneasy peace held until Henry VIII attempted to enthral Scotland by arranging for his son, Edward, to marry the infant Mary Queen of Scots. Henry was rebuffed and turned from pen to sword and the so-called Rough Wooing (1544–55). Meanwhile the Scots spirited Mary across the sea to

France where she married the French dauphin, the future François II. During Mary's reign the Scottish Reformation took place, when in 1560 John Knox laid before the Scottish parliament a Confession of Faith followed by a Book of Discipline, which decreed the organisation of the church and envisaged a scheme of education from primary school to university which was way ahead of its time.

It was preaching to the converted: St Andrews University had already been founded in 1411, followed by the universities of Glasgow (1451), Aberdeen (1494) and Edinburgh (1582) and, from the outset, Scottish education was meritocratic with the son of the ploughman sitting alongside the son of the laird. But it was not all work and no play, and by the 15th century golf was already being played and whisky drunk while shinty (legalised mayhem on a hockey field) and curling (lawn bowls played on ice) had long been enjoyed.

Every Man his own Church

James VI succeeded Mary and when the Union of the Crowns occurred in 1603 he was crowned James I of England. James believed in episcopacy – a church controlled by bishops appointed by the king – whereas more radical Protestants favoured Presbyterianism, in which authority resided with elders chosen by the congregation. Charles I, James' son, inherited his father's belief and attempted to introduce a new, much resented, prayer book, which led to Scots signing the National Covenant in 1638.

In 1643 the Solemn League and Covenant united the Covenanters and the English parliamentary party against Charles I. Many Covenanters, including the Marquess of Montrose, were torn between loyalty to the cause and to their king. Montrose opted for the latter and was defeated at Philliphaugh (1645) and exiled. Charles I was executed in 1649.

The Scots were dismayed and when the dead king's heir signed the Covenant even though 'Presbytery was not a religion for gentlemen' they crowned him Charles II. Once crowned he rejected his promises and restored episcopacy in 1661. The extreme Covenanters stuck to their guns and there followed years of savage suppression – the 'Killing Times' (1680s). The Covenanters, knowing they were predestined to grace, were not deterred and became all the more eager for martyrdom.

Charles II was succeeded in 1685 by Catholic James II (James VII of Scotland) who in the 'Glorious Revolution' of 1688 was ousted by his daughter Mary and her Protestant Dutch husband William of Orange. These two re-established Presbyterianism and Scotland was once again

James VI (James I of England)

The Covenanters opposed royal control of the Church

divided into supporters of the new order and supporters of the exiled James, who were called Jacobites. Confrontation occurred at the indecisive Battle of Killiecrankie (1689) after which William offered a pardon to those clan chiefs who would swear allegiance to him by 1 January 1692.

Most toed the line, but one chieftain, Alisdair MacDonald, arrived too late to take the oath. The government ordered Campbell troops, old enemies of the MacDonalds, to be billeted in the latter's cottages of Glencoe and then to kill all those aged under 70 as they lay in their beds. The Massacre of Glencoe in 1692 will always be a black day in Scottish history, not only because of the flow of red blood but because the Campbells violated a tradition of hospitality.

William's popularity was low, and was further eroded by the inability of Scottish traders to succeed in the face of privileged English competitors. The traders' response was the Darien Expedition, an attempt to found a merchant colony in Panama, which turned out to be the worst commercial undertaking in Scottish history: 2,000 lives were lost and the exchequer and the storehouses were left almost bare. Some now believed the only hope for economic success was equal trading rights with England. And so, in 1707, the Scottish Parliament, 'bought and sold for English gold', signed the Act of Union and adjourned; it did not reconvene until 1999. The Crown, the Sword and the Sceptre were placed in a box and forgotten until discovered by Walter Scott in the early 19th century. However, the Kirk (Church), the educational system, the law and the judicial system were preserved.

Meanwhile Jacobitism (the opposition) had reached its apogee in the 1715 rising. This owed little to the exiled court of James Francis Stuart (the 'Old Pretender'), the son of James VII, but was catalysed by the ambitions of the Earl of Mar. The rebellion ended with the indecisive Battle of Sheriffmuir which was fought even before the 'Old Pretender' landed.

Prince Charles and Flora MacDonald

Why the famous Jacobite insurrection of 1745, led by Bonnie Prince Charlie, occurred is a mystery. There was economic prosperity and few Scots supported the Jacobite cause. Still, Prince Charles Edward Stuart, son of the 'Old Pretender', had daring, ego and charisma and the concealed backing of the French. After conquering Scotland, Charlie confirmed his conquest by a victory at Prestonpans. But it all came undone and defeat at Culloden in 1746 was final. Charlie fled to a fugitive existence, in which he was aided by Flora MacDonald, before escaping to France. Jacobitism was dead.

Yet, Church polemics would persist and by the 19th century it seemed every Scot needed his own church. Matters came to a head with the Disruption in 1843, when Dr Thomas Chalmers marched out of the General Assembly of the Church of Scotland to form the Free Church of Scotland. Several other schisms occurred but in 1900 most of the splinter Presbyterian groups reunited to become the United Free Church, and in 1929 that church linked up with the Church of Scotland. However, the Wee Frees, a small minority mainly in the Hebrides, to whom the sabbath is utterly inviolate, remain independent. Add to the mix in what is now a fairly tolerant society, 77,500 Catholics and 57,000 Episcopalians.

Persecution and Enlightenment

Culloden signalled the end of the Highland way of life. The 1747 Act of Proscription – repealed in 1782 – banned Highland dress and the playing of bagpipes. Clan chieftains no longer felt responsibility for their clansmen but were more interested in the 'bottom line'. With fighting a thing of the past, the clansman could no longer pay his master with services, and his master, attracted by London, required cash. The answer was sheep. Tenants were evicted (Highland Clearances), leading to large-scale emigration. Samuel Johnson commented: 'to govern peaceably by having no subjects is an expedient that argues no great profundity of policy.' Today, 'evictions' continue with Scots being replaced by foreign, often English, incomers and sheep by red deer.

While the Highlands were depopulated, cities and industrial areas burgeoned. The population of about 1.5 million in 1800 had grown to nearly 5 million by 1911. An influx of Catholic Irish immigrants had been forced from their homes by the potato famine in Ireland.

Burns as a young man

Possibly because Presbyterianism placed such high value on education, the Scottish Enlightenment – approximately 1750–1850 – witnessed a remarkable explosion of intellectual life dominated by David Hume and Adam Smith, espousing respectively theories of philosophy and economics.

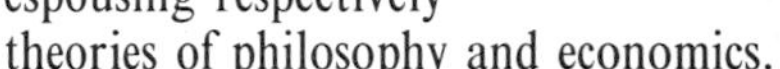

Distinguished contemporaries were the poet Allan Ramsay and his son, a portrait painter of the same name, and the architect Robert Adam. They were followed by the essayist Thomas Carlyle, the Nasmyths – father a painter, son an engineer – the painter David Wilkie and Robert Burns, Walter Scott and James Hogg, the 'Ettrick shepherd'. Scotland's contribution to the world was not only literary and philosophical: she also nurtured a steady stream of theoretical and practical scientific geniuses – Napier, Watt, Telford, Macadam, Bell, Lord Kelvin, Simpson, Lister, Logie Baird, Watson-Watt.

After the Union, Scotland began to prosper. By the 1750s there was a flourishing trade in the re-export of tobacco from America and a thriving linen industry. When these slumped they were replaced by cotton. The emphasis next shifted to heavy industry. Clydeside led the world in ship-building and locomotive manufacture and built over 43 different automobiles – and remained on top until after World War II. Today, wealth comes from oil, whisky, tourism and the electronic industries in 'Silicon Glen' in the Central Belt.

A Voice in their own Destiny

However, political life was almost at a standstill. Not until 1853 did a new Scottish nationalism manifest itself in the foundation of the National Association for Vindication of Scottish Rights. By 1880 this body was muttering about Home Rule and so in 1855

View of Edinburgh in 1812

The Scottish Parliament Building

the London government appointed a Secretary for Scotland with a Cabinet seat. In 1894 a Scottish Grand Committee comprising all Scotland's MPs was established, but it wasn't until 1927 that a Scottish Office was established in Edinburgh.

At this time Scotland provided a fertile breeding ground for the British Left. The Scottish Labour Party, founded in 1888, soon merged with the Independent Labour Party which played a major role in the formation of the (British) Labour Party. Britain's first Labour MP, Keir Hardie, and Britain's first Labour prime minister, Ramsay Macdonald, were both Scots; six British prime ministers in the 20th century have been Scots. The 1922 general election established an electoral pattern which has remained, with one exception, ever since: even when England returns a Conservative majority, Scotland votes Labour.

The post-war depression hit Scotland hard, leading to a revival of the Home Rule Movement and the founding in 1932 of the Scottish National Party (SNP). The party reached its apogee in the 1970s with 11 MPs at Westminster (out of a total of 635). A 1979 referendum proposing a form of devolution was rejected, but in the 1990s the desire among Scots to run their own affairs rose again. In September 1997, shortly after the election of the first Labour government since 1979, another referendum voted overwhelmingly in favour of the re-establishment of a Scottish Parliament. In the 1997 general election, out of 72 Scottish MPs, not one Conservative had been returned.

Through the 1980s and 1990s, the Liberals and their successors the Liberal Democrats won considerable support in Scotland and held a number of Scottish seats, with particular strongholds in the Borders and the north-east. Elections to the new Scottish Parliament, held in May 1999 with proportional representation (a system new to the UK), resulted in a coalition Labour and Liberal Democrat government led by Labour's Donald Dewar. The Scottish Executive has the power to vary UK taxes, budgetary control and policy control over most but not all domestic affairs. Based in Edinburgh, it will convene in the Church of Scotland Assembly Hall until a costly, controversial new building has been completed at Holyrood.

Historical Highlights

432 St Ninian founds a Christian church at Whithorn in the south-west of Scotland.

563 Landing of St Columba on Iona followed by conversion of Picts to Christianity.

843 Kenneth MacAlpin becomes the first king to rule over both the Scots and the Picts.

1057 King Macbeth is slain but nowhere near either Birnam Wood or Dunsinane.

1297 William Wallace leads first Scottish rebellion and defeats English at Stirling Bridge.

1314 Robert Bruce defeats English at Bannockburn and restores independence to Scotland.

1411 Foundation of first Scottish university at St Andrews.

1542 Birth of Mary Queen of Scots.

1560 John Knox inspires Protestant Reformation.

1561 Mary returns to Scotland after spending 13 years in France and becoming Queen of France.

1603 Union of the Crowns with accession of James VI to the throne of England.

1638 Signing of the National Covenant in Edinburgh by which the signatories pledged 'to defend their religious liberties'.

1665 Jews begin to settle in tolerant Scotland.

1690 Presbyterian Church is irrevocably established.

1695 Bank of Scotland is founded by William Paterson who also founded the Bank of England.

1707 The Union of Scottish and English parliaments is ill-received in Scotland.

1719 General Wade builds road to control the Highlands after the 1715 Jacobite rising.

1745 The Jacobite rising under Bonnie Prince Charlie ends at Culloden in 1746.

1759 Birth of Robert Burns.

1765 James Watt invents steam engine in Glasgow and the Industrial Revolution is born.

1840 Highland Clearances: forced emigration of crofters to make way for sheep farms, later succeeded by deer forests.

1843 The Disruption: secession of ministers and members of the Established Church to form the Free Church of Scotland.

1847 Chloroform first used by Simpson in Edinburgh.

1860 World's first professional golf tournament held at Prestwick.

1865 Lister introduces antiseptic surgery in Glasgow.

1871 Idea of chain stores probably originated in Scotland with Lipton and Bishop, Glasgow grocers.

1876 Alexander Graham Bell, an Edinburgh native, transmits the first coherent message on a telephone.

1883 Boys Brigade founded in Glasgow by Wm Alexander Smith.

1924 Ramsay MacDonald, a Scot, becomes Britain's first Labour Prime Minister.

1928 Helensburgh-born John Logie Baird gives first public demonstration of television.

1932 National Party of Scotland (SNP) formed.

1947 Edinburgh International Festival and Edinburgh Military Tattoo inaugurated.

1964–1970s Development of North Sea oil and gas fields.

1967 Winifred Ewing, first SNP member, elected to Parliament.

1974 Eleven SNP MPs are elected.

1975 First oil pumped ashore from North Sea pipelines.

1979 Referendum on proposed Assembly fails to bring about partial devolution from England.

1997 The Stone of Destiny on which Scottish kings were once crowned is returned to Scotland. National referendum votes for a Scottish Parliament with tax-varying powers.

1998 The Museum of Scotland opens in Edinburgh, the new parliamentary capital.

1999 First elections to the Scottish Parliament result in a Labour/Liberal Democrat Coalition, with Donald Dewar as First Minister.

Scotland
32 km / 20 miles
ATLANTIC OCEAN
NORTH SEA
Shetland Islands
Unst
Yell
Papa Stour
Shetland Mainland
Foula
Lerwick
Sumburgh
Fair Isle
Westray
Sanday
Rousay
Stronsay
Orkney Mainland
Shapinsay
Stromness
Kirkwall
Hoy & West Mainland
Hoy
Orkney Islands
Pentland Firth
Dunnet Head
Duncansby Head
John o'Groats
Thurso
Melvich
Wick
Lybster
Helmsdale
Cape Wrath
Durness
Kyle of Tongue
Tongue
Ben Hope 927
Naver
North-west Sutherland
Scourie
Eddrachillis Bay
Altnaharra
Loch Shin
Ben More Assynt 998
Enard Bay
Assynt-Coigach
Lairg
Ullapool
Dornoch Firth
Royal Dornoch
Dornoch
Tarbat Ness
Tain
Moray Firth
NORTH WEST HIGHLANDS
Gairloch
Wester Ross
Loch Maree
Garve
Achnasheen
Dingwall
Cromarty
Nairn
Inverness
Elgin
Buckie
Banff
Macduff
Kinnaird Head
Fraserburgh
Peterhead
Cruden Bay
Ellon
Royal Aberdeen
Inverurie
Don
Aberdeenshire
Huntly
Moray
Spey
Grantown-on-Spey
Aviemore
CAIRNGORM MOUNTAINS
Loch Ness
Fort Augustus
Glen Strathfarrar
Highland
Glen Affric
Kintail
Knoydart
Kyle of Lochalsh
Armadale
Inner Sound
Trotternish
Uig
Loch Snizort
Portree
Skye
The Cuillin Hills
Rum
Canna
The Minch
Butt of Lewis
Port of Ness
Stornoway
Lewis
South Lewis, Harris & North Uist
Tarbert
Harris
Outer Hebrides
North Uist
Lochmaddy
Benbecula
South Uist
South Uist Machair
Lochboisdale
Barra

Sea
Inner Hebride
Eigg
Muck
Coll
Tiree
Lochailort
Morar, Moidart & Ardnamurchan
Loch Shiel
Fort William
Ben Nevis 1344
Dalwhinnie
GRAMPIAN MOUNTAINS
Deeside & Lochnagar
Stonehaven
Inverbervie
Angus
Brechin
Montrose
Forfar
Arbroath
Blair Atholl
Loch Rannoch
Loch Tummel
Pitlochry
Loch Rannoch & Glen Lyon
Perthshire and Kinross
Blairgowrie
Dundee
Carnoustie
Firth of Tay
Tobermory
Lochaline
Ben Nevis & Glen Coe
Ben Lawers 1214
Loch Tay
Tay
Loch na Keal
Mull
Lynn of Lorn
Bridge of Orchy
Oban
Fionnphort
Argyll and Bute
Crianlarich
Crieff
Perth
Gleneagles
St Andrews
Firth of Lorn
Loch Awe
Inveraray
Stirling
The Trossachs
Ben Lomond 973
OCHIL HILLS
M 90
Fife
Fife Ness
Crail
Colonsay
Tarbet
Forth
Glenrothes
Loch Lomond
Stirling
Dunfermline
Firth of Forth
Kirkcaldy
North Berwick
Lochgilphead
Jura
Knapdale
Kyles of Bute
Greenock
Dumbarton
Falkirk
Grangemouth
M 9
Muirfield
Dunbar
St. Abb's Head
Clydebank
Livingston
EDINBURGH
East Lothian
Kennacraig
Islay
Bute
Paisley
Glasgow
Airdrie
M 8
Midlothian
Berwick-upon-Tweed
Motherwell
KINTYRE
North Ayrshire
East Kilbride
Wishaw
Borders
Lindisfarne or Holy Is.
Tweed
Ardrossan
Clyde
Lanark
Peebles
Galashiels
Irvine
Kilmarnock
M 74
Upper Tweeddale
Arran
Troon
East Ayrshire
South Lanarkshire
Selkirk
Wooler
Embleton
Prestwick
Abington
Jedburgh
Rathlin Island
Campbeltown
Ayr
Firth of Clyde
Hawick
Alnwick
North Channel
Sanquhar
Moffat
CHEVIOT HILLS
Mull of Kintyre
Turnberry
Girvan
South Ayrshire
Otterburn
L. Foyle
Coleraine
Nith
Langholm
Northumberland
Londonderry
Ballantrae
Galloway Forest
Dumfries and Galloway
A 74(M)
NORTHERN IRELAND
Newton Stewart
Dumfries
Cairnryan
Castle Douglas
Nith Estuary
Gretna Green
Brampton
N. Tyne
Hexham
Newcastle upon Tyne
South Shields
Larne
Stranraer
East Stewartry Coast
Carlisle
Sunderland
Gatehouse of Fleet
Solway Firth
M 6
ENGLAND
A 1(M)
Bangor
Cumbria
Durham
Lough Neagh
BELFAST
Newtownards
Workington
Penrith
Durham
Lake District

Day itiner

All the itineraries I've put together in the following pages assume you will be based in Edinburgh, which is a compact city. In Edinburgh you don't need a car: distances are short, taxis are many and public transport is excellent. Itineraries outside Edinburgh are described on the understanding that a car is used. In the Highlands you might find yourself on single-lane roads with clearly indicated passing places: in such circumstances be courteous and be prepared to reverse.

After three full-day itineraries – Edinburgh, Glasgow, and Stirling and the Trossachs – which are my three essential snapshots of Scotland, I've arranged several half-day itineraries in and around Edinburgh and two additional full-day excursions. Finally, I've suggested a two-day excursion including the West Highlands and the Isle of Skye. For all itineraries you should be at the starting point at 9am or 2pm. For routes which take you beyond Edinburgh – Glasgow, Stirling and the Trossachs, the Borders, Crieff, St Andrews and Fife – you should set off from your Edinburgh hotel at about 8am. You should also be prepared to leave at this time on your two-day excursion.

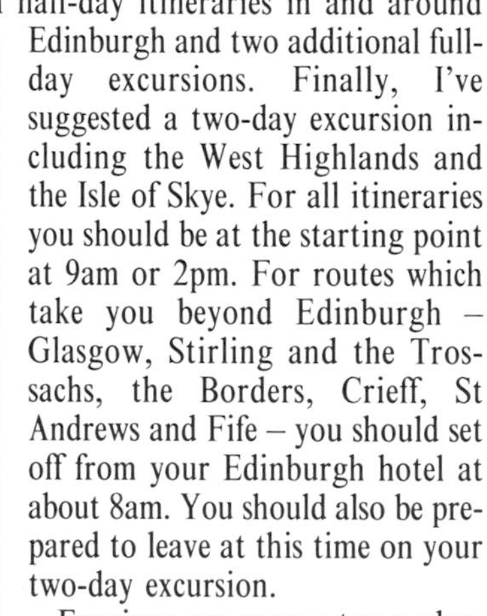

Evenings are yours; try a play, a concert, the Edinburgh Tattoo during the Festival, a Scottish evening and/or a nightclub, all of which are listed in the Nightlife and Calendar sections of this book.

Edinburgh's New Town

As it used to be

Edinburgh

A 60-minute bus tour will provide a quick once-over of the city. Follow this by a visit to the Castle, a stroll down the Royal Mile with its many historical sites, and a visit to the Palace of Holyrood House.

– To the start: bus tours originate just off Princes Street outside the entrance to Waverley Station on Waverley Bridge. After the tour it is a 10-minute walk or taxi ride to the Castle –

The first **Edinburgh Classic Tour** (tel: 0131-554 4494) of the day departs shortly after 9am (later in winter) and thereafter runs every 15 minutes. The tours last about one hour. Passengers may alight as often as they like and reboard a later bus. After the tour you might wish to adjourn to the **Acanthus** immediately across the road, for morning coffee, before setting off up the hill.

The present **Edinburgh Castle** (April to September: daily 9.30am–5.15pm last entry; rest of year: daily 9.30am–4.15pm last entry; tel: 0131-225 1012) was built between the 14th and 16th centuries but a castle has stood here for at least 1,000 years and the earliest surviving part – St Margaret's chapel – dates from *circa* 1100.

On crossing the drawbridge, notice the statues of Robert the Bruce and Sir William Wallace, heroes who fought the English. Follow the signs to 'Citadel', but detour to visit the vaults where French prisoners were held

Edinburgh Castle

Castle guard

during the Napoleonic Wars. They now house Mons Meg, a giant cannon forged in 1449. The terrace fronting the tiny chapel provides superb panoramas of Edinburgh.

From here use the Esplanade entrance to enter **Crown Square**, the hub of today's castle, and visit the Palace or King's Lodging, the Great Hall, and the Scottish War Museum. The Palace has a tiny room where Mary Queen of Scots gave birth to the future James VI of Scotland and I of England, and the Crown Room houses the Regalia (crown jewels) of Scotland. Nearby sits the recently repatriated Stone of Destiny, on which Scottish kings once stood to be crowned. The bare Great Hall with its hammerbeam roof was built by James IV early in the 16th century and once housed the Scottish Parliament. It now contains the armoury. As you leave the **Castle Esplanade** a plaque on the left marks a fountain where more than 300 people, thought to be witches, were executed between 1479 and 1722.

Beyond the Esplanade four streets – Castlehill, Lawnmarket, High Street, and Canongate – make up the **Royal Mile** which runs right down from the Castle to the Palace of Holyrood House. Grey 17th-century houses, their facades pierced by narrow, dark, foreboding

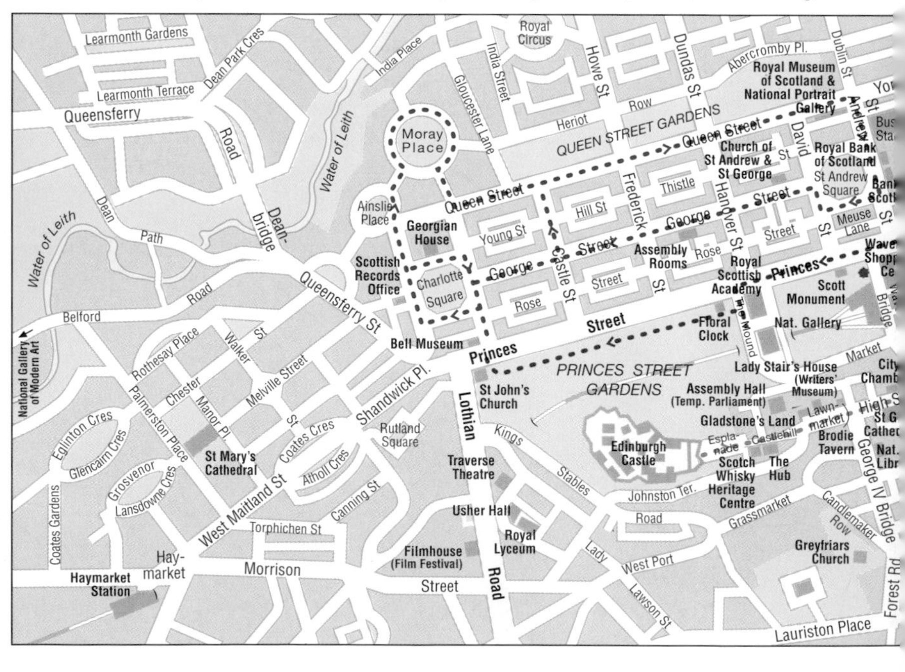

Deacon Brodie's Tavern

closes (entrances), line both sides. Enter any of these and you will find courtyards, many of which have steep steps or precipitous slopes leading to streets below.

History of a different variety can be enjoyed if you visit the **Scotch Whisky Heritage Centre** just down from the castle (daily 10am–6pm, last tour 5pm; extended hours in summer; tel: 0131-220 0441) which unfolds the story of the *guid stuff* through 300 years of history. Or if you want solid sustenance, step into **The Jolly Judge** at 7 St James Court for a pleasant pub lunch, or the café at **The Hub Festival Centre** in the old Tolbooth Kirk, where if it's festival time you can also buy tickets to events.

Walk down into the Lawnmarket and cross the street to **Gladstone's Land** (April to October: Monday to Saturday 10am–5pm, Sunday 2–5pm; tel: 0131-226 5856), a narrow six-storey tenement typical of the 17th century. In tenements language a 'land' is a house and a 'house' is a flat or apartment. The premises behind the pavement arcade have been fully restored as a ground-floor shop with living quarters on the upper floor. Notice the painted ceilings, fireplaces and glorious 17th-century furniture.

A short close descends to **Lady Stair's House** (Monday to Saturday 10am–5pm; Sundays during the Festival 2–5pm; tel: 0131-529 4901) whose former owner, a 17th-century beauty, gave her name to what is now the Writers' Museum, devoted to memorabilia of Scotland's three great literary figures – Burns, Scott and Stevenson.

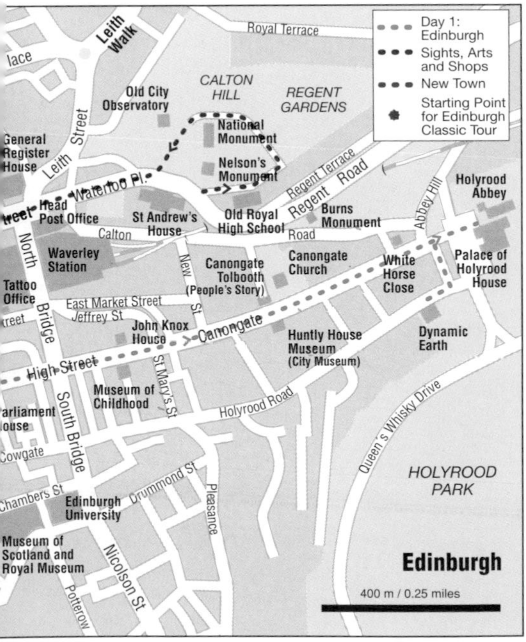

At the corner of Lawnmarket and George IV Bridge, opposite the Scottish Parliament Visitor Centre, you can stop for refreshment at **Deacon Brodie's Tavern**. William Brodie, a respected citizen by day, and a rogue by night,

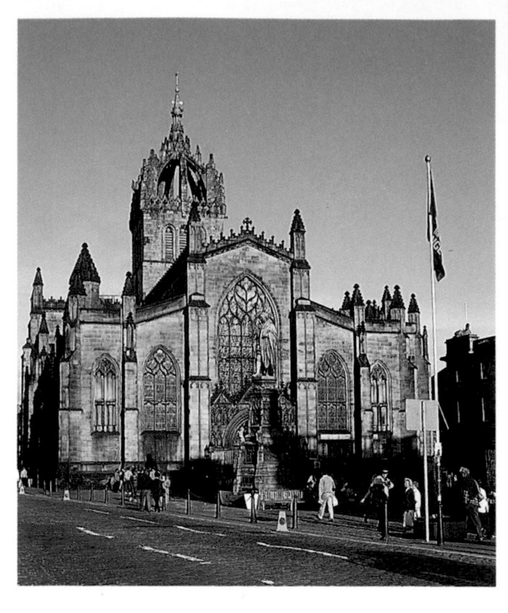

St Giles Cathedral

was born across the road in Brodie Close and was hanged just outside the tavern on new gallows he had designed. He was the inspiration for Stevenson's *Dr Jekyll and Mr Hyde*. This marks the end of the Lawnmarket: across the busy intersection of Bank Street and George IV Bridge is High Street.

Parliament Square, on the right, is occupied by **St Giles Cathedral** (winter: Monday to Saturday 9am–5pm and Sunday 1–5pm; summer: Monday to Friday 9am–7pm, Saturday 9am–5pm, Sunday 1–5pm; tel: 0131-225 9442) and is surrounded by public buildings with Parliament Hall and the Signet Library (closed to the public) being of most interest. Although a church has stood here since 854 the oldest part of the present edifice is the four massive central pillars which date from around 1120. The church is irrevocably connected with the Scottish Reformation (1560s) and the name 'cathedral' is something of a misnomer. That dates from 1633 when Charles I introduced bishops to the Presbyterian church and although the bishop was removed by the end of that century, by which time Presbyterianism had been re-established, the honorific title stuck. Other than the distinctive 15th-century crowned tower topped with a gold weather-vane, the exterior is undistinguished; inside it's a different matter. Outstanding is the Thistle Chapel (1911) with an angel playing bagpipes carved on the entrance arch and an impressively-ornamented Gothic interior.

The small heart-shaped arrangement of cobblestones to the left of the front (west) door is known as **Heart of Midlothian**. It marks the site of a 14th-century Tolbooth which was demolished in 1817 after serving at different times as the home of the Scottish Parliament, a Court of Law and a jail. From its latter use stems the tradition that it is lucky to spit upon this spot where a grid stood over the heads of condemned prisoners.

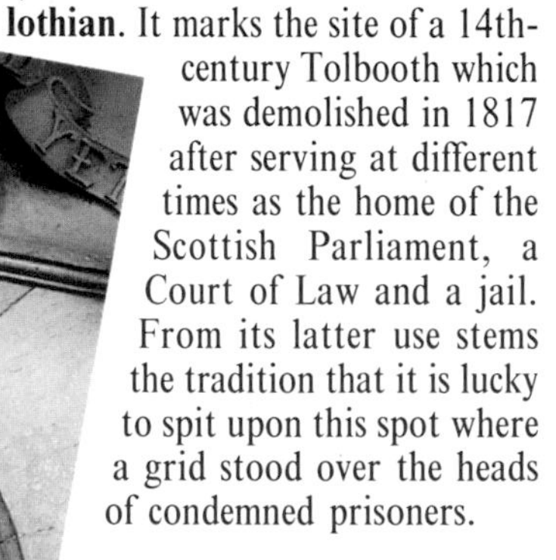

On the Royal Mile

Incorporated in the shaft of the **Mercat Cross** at the east end of St Giles is part of the original 15th-century cross. This was a meeting place in the medieval city and the venue for executions, royal proclamations and other celebrations.

Cross the square and enter **Parliament Hall** (Monday to Friday 9am–5pm; tel: 0131-225 2595) and be greeted by a superb hammerbeam roof, a roaring fire, a brilliant great window showing the inauguration of the Court of Session in 1532 by James V and portraits of celebrated lawyers. The Scottish Parliament met here between 1639 and 1707 and the building is now home to the Court of Session, Edinburgh's legal heart. The statue of Charles II in front of the building dates from 1685 and is the oldest equestrian statue in Britain.

Across the road, fronted by a stone screen, are the **City Chambers,** built between 1753 and 1761 as the Royal Exchange. Alongside is **Anchor Close**, which is steeped in 18th-century literary traditions. Here stood the Anchor Tavern, a favourite pub of Robert Burns; the printing works of William Smellie who in 1768 published the first edition of the *Encyclopedia Brittanica* and in 1787 the first Edinburgh edition of Burns's poems; and the home of the parents of Sir Walter Scott (Scott himself lived in the Borders – *see Excursion 1, page 55*).

Cross the junction of North Bridge and South Bridge. (If you have not yet had lunch, the **Royal Mile Tavern** serves a good pub meal.) Beckoning are the chimneys, red tiled roof and crow-step gable of the picturesque **John Knox House** – built *circa* 1490 and now with several additions – which is the outstanding example of an Edinburgh town house of this period. Knox, the Protestant reformer, is believed to have lived here from 1561 to 1572 (Monday to Saturday 10am–5pm; Sundays in August noon–5pm; tel: 0131-556 2647).

The gabled John Knox House

Next to the house is the **Netherbow Arts Centre** (tel: 0131-556 9579), comprising a small theatre, galleries and a restaurant, styled as an old Edinburgh town house and opened in 1972 as the Arts Centre of the Church of Scotland. A few steps further along, brass plates set in the roadway at the junction of St Mary's Street and Jeffrey Street, mark the outline of the last **Netherbow Port**, one of six gates to the old city of Edinburgh. Heads of criminals and preachers were exhibited on spikes above the gate, the preachers' between their hands with palms displayed in the attitude of prayer.

Cross the road and backtrack a few yards to the **Museum of Childhood** (free entry; Monday to Saturday 10am–5pm; Sundays during the Festival 2–5pm; tel: 0131-529 4142) with its dolls, games and innumerable other items from bygone days.

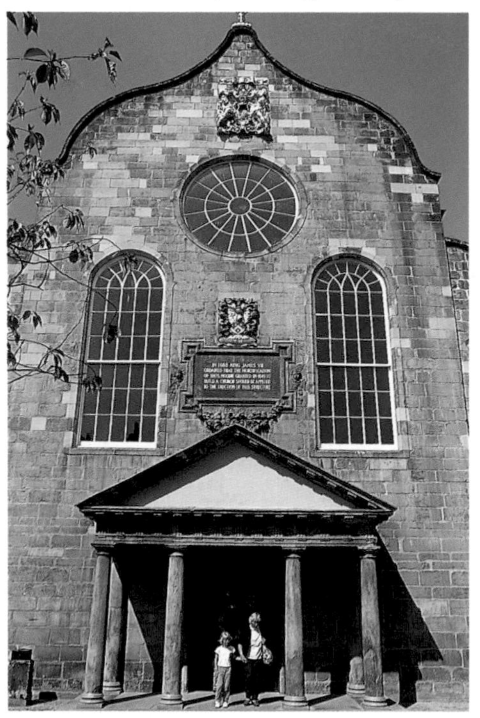

Canongate Church

The Royal Mile now becomes Canongate, whose name derives from the canons or clerics of Holyrood Abbey and 'gait' – a walk or road. Aristocrats once lived here, close to Holyrood Palace. The 1592 **Canongate Tolbooth** is easily recognised with its Franco-Scottish turrets and projecting clock. Scottish tolbooths were civic centres that held the jail. It now houses the superb **People's Story** (free entry; Monday to Saturday 10am–5pm; Sundays during the Festival 2–5pm; tel: 0131-529 4057) whose sounds, smells and models recall the lives of ordinary Edinburgh people since the late 18th century.

The equally excellent **Huntly House Museum** (free entry; Monday to Saturday 10am–5pm; Sundays during the Festival 2–5pm; tel: 0131-529 4143) is immediately across the road. It is an amalgamation of several 1570 town houses, with two projecting floors of plastered timber. This is Edinburgh's main museum of local history, with displays including splendid collections of silver and glass and the National Covenant of 1638 signed as a protest against Charles I's attempts to establish episcopacy and to introduce a new prayer book in Scotland.

Across the road is the Dutch-looking **Canongate Kirk** which was built in 1688 when James VII ousted the congregation from Holyrood Abbey, which he converted to a chapel for members of the

Order of the Thistle. At this point you could stop for afternoon tea at **Clarinda's**, a small, delightful traditional Scottish tearoom with great home baking, a Scottish speciality.

Beyond this, a plaque on the wall of Jenny Ha's pub marks Golfer's Land, which was built by John Paterson, a shoemaker, with winnings from a golf match when he partnered the Duke of York (later King James VII). A short distance further down and reached from under an arcade, the tastefully restored **White Horse Close** is worth more than a glance. The Royal Mews was situated here in the 16th century and from 1623 it was the site of the White Horse Inn and coaching stables from where the stagecoach left for London.

Refreshments available

Note at this point, in the middle of the road, a small circle of cobblestones. These marked the western limits of the sanctuary of Holyrood which, until 1880, offered refuge to debtors who were known as 'Abbey lairds'. The Girth Cross which stood here was the site of proclamations and many executions. Women's Lib was unknown when, in 1600, beautiful Lady Warrison was decapitated for conspiring to murder her husband who had cruelly mistreated her. Her maid was also convicted and burned on Castle Hill.

And so to the **Palace of Holyrood House**, which was originally a guest house for visitors to Holyrood Abbey but which gradually grew in importance. The oldest remaining section is the north tower (to the left as you look at the front of the building) which was built in the 16th century for James IV. The remainder of the building is 17th century and includes a second tower, mirroring the old one. If any one place is associated with Mary Queen of Scots then this is it. Here, during six tumultuous years, she quarrelled with John Knox, married Darnley and Boswell, her second and third husbands, saw her secretary David Rizzio murdered, and was taken from here to captivity in Loch Leven castle. Later, in 1745, Bonnie Prince Charlie held court here

Holyrood Palace

Royal Crest at Holyrood Palace

and in 1822 it was the headquarters of George IV during his hilarious state visit. The Palace is the official residence of the Queen when she visits Scotland, and as a working palace it is occasionally closed (open daily from April to October 9.30am–5.15pm last entry; November to March 9.30am–3.45pm last entry; tel: 0131-556 1096).

Visitors are led on 40-minute guided tours through a series of 17th-century State Rooms whose most notable features are Flemish and French furniture and tapestries and magnificent intricate plasterwork ceilings. Then comes the Great Gallery with 87 paintings of supposed Scottish kings – and Mary. These are by a Dutchman, Jacob de Wit. Next visited are the historical apartments in the 16th-century northwest tower. From Darnley's rooms on one floor a narrow stairway leads to Mary's on the second floor. Outstanding are the wooden ceilings, one of which is divided into 16 panels recalling the 'auld alliance' between Scotland and France. The exit from the Palace leads to the now roofless 12th–13th-century **Abbey** where the remains of several Scottish kings are interred. Here, too, Mendelssohn composed the first 16 bars of his *Scottish Symphony*.

From nearby Queen's Drive, the energetic can walk to the top of Arthur's Seat (823ft/250m), where, when it was covered in wild forest, Mary hunted boar, and from where there are grand panoramic views of the city. Such an excursion was recommended by no less a sightseer than Sir Walter Scott in *Heart of Midlothian*. Alternatively, take a look at the redevelopment in progress on Holyrood Road (parallel to Canongate on the south side), including the parliament site and new offices of *The Scotsman* newspaper. If you have children with you, visit Edinburgh's answer to London's Millennium Dome, **Dynamic Earth** (Easter to October daily 10am–6pm; November to Easter, Wednesday to Sunday 10am–5pm; tel: 0131-550 7800).

For your evening meal, try one of the restaurants recommended in the section on *Eating Out, pages 72–4*.

DAY 2

Glasgow

A visit to Scotland's most populous city and Edinburgh's great rival.

– To the start: leave the west end of Edinburgh on the A8 and at the Newbridge roundabout take the Glasgow motorway (M8) exiting, after 44 miles (70km) at the Charing Cross turn off. On exiting stay in the right lane and just before the first traffic light make a U-turn at the Glasgow University sign. Get into the left lane and after 200yds (183m) take the second turn on the left, a short hill which swings right to arrive at the equestrian statue of Field Marshal Lord Roberts, the hero of the Crimean War –

Glasgow's Conservation Area

You are now at the summit of the **Park Conservation Area**, described as 'the finest piece [in Britain] of architectural planning of the mid-19th century' and offering views to the west across the greenery of Kelvingrove Park. From this vantage point you can admire **Glasgow University** and glimpse three museums (all free) that are each well

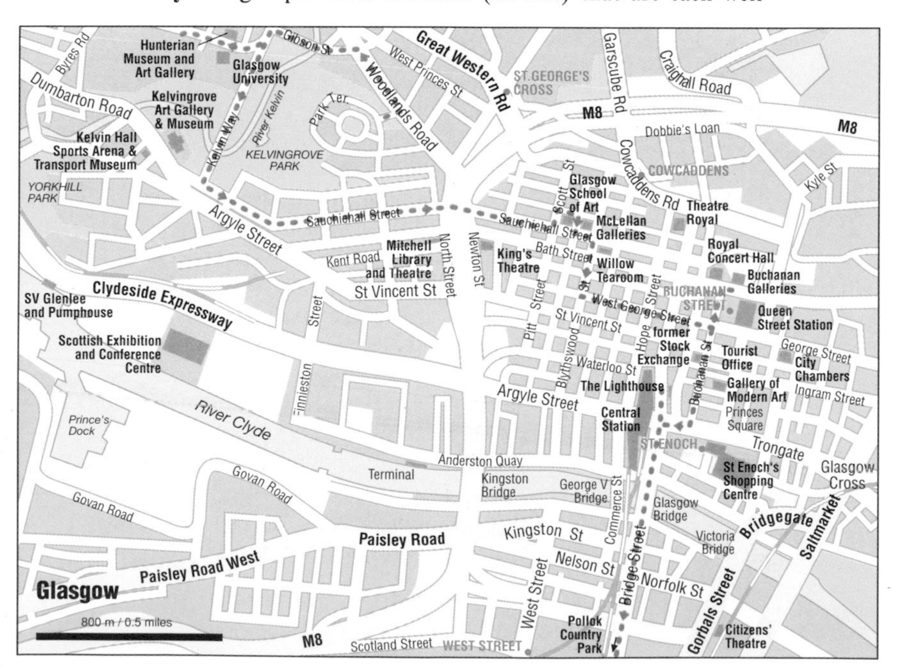

worth a visit – the Kelvingrove Art Gallery and Museum (Monday to Saturday 10am–5pm, Friday from 11am in winter; Sunday 11am–5pm; tel: 0141-287 2699), the Museum of Transport (hours as Kelvingrove; tel: 0141-287 2692) and the Hunterian Art Gallery (9.30am–5pm; closed Sunday; Mackintosh House closed 12.30–1.30pm; tel: 0141-330 5431). You will need to decide whether to 'do' all three lightly or visit one and reserve some time for either the Gallery of Modern Art or The Lighthouse later in the itinerary.

But first explore the Conservation Area. **Park Terrace**, immediately behind the belvedere, is possibly the most magnificent of all the terraces in the area. Stroll along Park Gate which bisects the Terrace and reach Park Circus, some of whose buildings are university halls of residence. Continue a few yards to the four towers which, from a distance, evoke images of a sun-kissed hill town in Italy. From here, turn back to the belvedere and to your car.

To reach the museums return to the main road and turn left. At the fork immediately ahead keep left and at the summit of the hill, reached after another 200yds (183m), turn left again. Glasgow University and the Hunterian are at the top of University Avenue, which is on your right. To reach the Kelvingrove Gallery keep straight – you are now driving through Kelvingrove Park – and, at the end of the park, after 400yds (366m), stands the massive red sandstone pile that is your destination.

Kelvingrove Gallery, with a pleasant tearoom, probably has the outstanding civic art collection in Britain. Important paintings from all European schools, especially the Dutch and late French, but also British, are well represented. Outstanding canvases are Rembrandt's *Man in Armour* and Rubens' *Nature Adorned by the Graces*. British painters are to the fore with particular emphasis on the 'Glasgow Boys' and 'Scottish Colourists'. Also on display are works of the new wave of internationally acclaimed Glasgow artists. Other galleries house displays of Decorative and Fine Arts, Natural History and Archaeology and Ethnography.

Immediately across the road is the **Museum of Transport**, which is arguably the best of its kind in Britain. Glasgow and the Clyde built not only ships and steam locomotives but also, at one time or another, aeroplanes and airships, motorcars and motorcycles,

Kelvingrove Gallery

In the Museum of Transport

and their fleet of tramcars was the envy of the world. Examples of all of these can be enjoyed.

(If you have opted to visit the Hunterian and want coffee beforehand, continue for a further 200yds/ 183m on University Avenue to Byres Road, probably the busiest shopping street outside the city centre, and the **Patisserie Françoise** at 138a, tel: 0141-334 1882.)

The **Hunterian Art Gallery**, entered through handsome doors by Eduardo Paolozzi, is part of Glasgow University and has an outstanding collection, not only of paintings by, but also of the painting equipment, furniture, silver and porcelain belonging to James McNeill Whistler. A longitudinal letter box in a door outside the gallery correctly suggests **Charles Rennie Mackintosh**, Glasgow's famous designer and architect. The door is part of a reconstruction of three levels of the nearby home in which the Mackintoshes lived, containing original pieces of Mackintosh furniture.

Museum visiting over for the present, drive eastwards towards the city, along Sauchiehall Street and past Charing Cross for slightly over one mile. (Those departing for the city from the Hunterian should return down University Avenue, then turn into Kelvingrove Park, then left onto Sauchiehall Street.) Now turn left on very steep Scott Street and arrive at the **Glasgow School of Art**, the *chef-d'oeuvre* of Mackintosh. The building can be admired from the outside though conducted tours are run from the school's **Mackintosh Shop** (weekdays 11am and 2pm; Saturday 10.30am and 11.30am; additional weekend tours in July and August; tel: 0141-353 4526). Nearby, at 217 Sauchiehall Street, is the **Willow Tearoom** (the ground floor is a jeweller's), the only remaining origi-

The School of Art

Look up for Glasgow style

nal Mackintosh tearoom: it is invariably busy and quite pricey.

Stroll south on Blythswood Street which immediately passes through Blythswood Square. Turn left into West George Street and, six blocks away, beckoning from Mandela Square, is St George's Tron church. Skirt the church, passing on the right the former Glasgow Stock Exchange, and then turn right. You are now in pedestrianised Buchanan Street, now dominated at its northern end by the big, new Buchanan Galleries shopping centre. The point of this stroll – less than one mile if you don't divert to the Buchanan Galleries – is that it is simpler than searching for a parking space and walking provides the opportunity to view some of the city's incomparable Victorian buildings, symbols of an imperial and mercantile past when Glasgow was the second city of the British empire.

Lunch at Princes Square

You might wish to stroll through a very short thoroughfare on the left which leads to Exchange Square whose centrepiece is the beautiful Stirling Building, once the home of one of Glasgow's tobacco barons and now housing the **Gallery of Modern Art** (free entry; Monday to Saturday 10am–5pm, Friday from 11am in winter; Sunday 11am–5pm; tel 0141-229 1996). Opened in 1996, its collection of paintings, sculpture and installations by living artists from around the world is still growing. Outside, on the square, **The Jenny** is a traditional Glasgow tearoom where you can enjoy a pleasant lunch.

Alternatively, the **Princes Square** shopping complex, featuring more historic architecture, is choc-a-bloc with eateries. A favourite is the relaxed rooftop **October Café**. After lunch, if time permits before visiting the Burrell Collection, continue southwards for 150yds (135m) and either cross Argyle Street to arrive at Europe's largest glass-covered mall, **St Enoch Shopping Centre** – where two floors of shopping should open the purse-strings if you have not already succumbed – or turn right along Argyle Street then first right into Mitchell Street for **The Lighthouse**. This is another Mackintosh building, recently converted into an architecture and design centre with displays on the master's work (Monday to Saturday 10.30am–6pm, except Tuesday from 11am and Thursday till 8pm; Sunday noon–5pm; tel: 0141-221 6362).

Return to the car for the journey to the internationally-acclaimed Burrell Collection (free entry; Monday to Saturday 10am– 5pm; Sunday, and Friday in winter, 11am– 5pm; tel: 0141-287 2550). From where you are parked make for Bridge Street and then drive straight for 2½ miles (4km) until arriving at a busy intersection: a fork in the road faces you: take the right arm and drive for a further mile, at which point the sign **Pollok Country Park (Burrell Collection)** appears on the right. Housed in an award-winning building that some say outshines the collection itself is a selection of the 8,000 treasures that Sir William Burrell, a Glasgow shipowner, bequeathed to his native city. Chinese ceramics and bronzes, ancient Mediterranean artefacts, Persian carpets, medieval tapestries, stained glass and furniture, Dutch and French paintings and sculpture all demand attention.

Pollok Country Park

Rather than immediately leaving the park stroll towards Pollok House – a distance of about ½ mile (800m) – passing en route Glasgow's prize-winning herd of Highland cattle. **Pollok House** (April to October daily 10am–5pm; November to March daily 11am–4pm; tel: 0141-616 6410) contains a fine collection of Spanish paintings together with furniture, ceramics and silver, and is set in beautiful gardens, with the river and a golf course beyond. Both the Burrell and Pollok House have pleasant tearooms.

To return to Edinburgh, turn left when you leave the park and after one mile pick up the M8 motorway. Alternatively, you could try the recommendations for a Glaswegian evening in *Nightlife, pages 76–79,* and *Eating Out, pages 74–5.*

Stirling and the Trossachs

A visit to Stirling, the 'Gateway to the Highlands', and its castle, followed by an exploration of the Trossachs and Loch Lomond.

– To the start: leave the west end of Edinburgh on the A8 and at the Newbridge roundabout take the M9 motorway for Stirling, a distance of 37 miles (60km) –

On entering **Stirling** drive directly to the **Castle** (April to September: daily 9.30am–5.15pm last entry; rest of year: daily 9.30am–4.15pm last entry; tel: 01786-431 316) and, after watching an audiovisual presentation in the Visitor Centre on the Esplanade, enjoy a guided tour of this historic building, long the favourite residence of the Stuart monarchy. James II and V were born here and Mary Queen of Scots and James VI spent time here.

Admire the palace, which James V had built around a central courtyard and which is one of Scotland's renaissance glories. The most striking feature of this building, with ornate stonework largely cut by French craftsmen, is the exterior facade. The castle's chapel was built on the instructions of James VI while the 125-ft (38-m) Great Hall or Parliament House, with its exquisite carving and tracery, dates from James IV; its 9-year restoration to its 16th-century splendour, including the repainting of the Great Hall, was recently completed. Superb views can be enjoyed from the spot

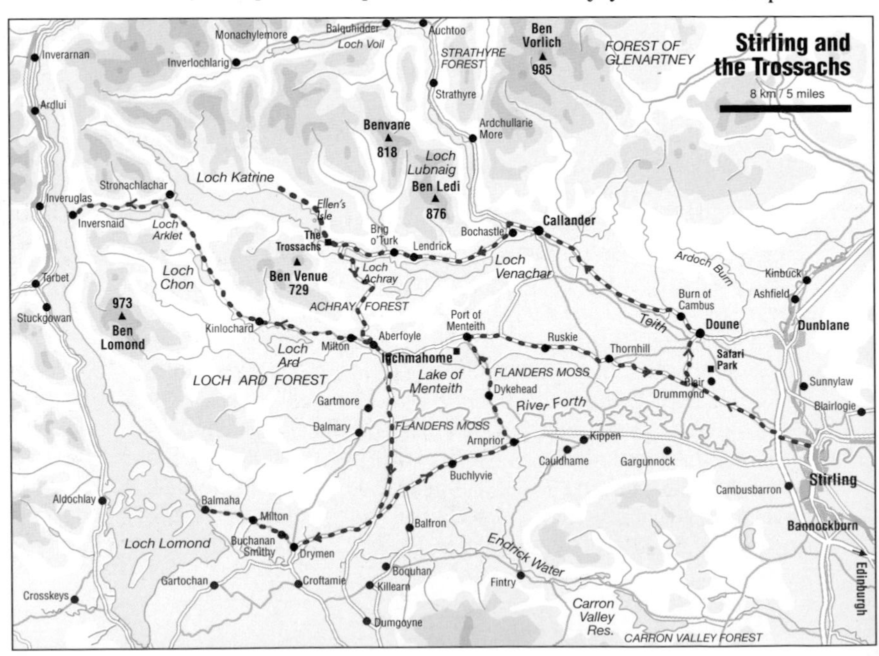

Stirling Castle

where, at the northwest corner of the castle ramparts, Queen Victoria once gazed across a balustrade which still bears her initials.

Once you've seen the castle go down to **Darnley's Coffee House** at 18 Bow Street for a fine selection of home-baked goodies as well as wines and beers.

Leave Stirling northwards on the Crianlarich (A84) road; at the M9 roundabouts take the 2nd and then 3rd exits. Cross the River Forth into farmland and after 3 miles (5km), you will see a sign for **Blair Drummond Safari and Leisure Park** (April to September 10am–4.30pm last entry; tel: 01786-841 456). This is Scotland's only safari park, and it has lions, tigers, giraffes and elephants. A further 2 miles (4km), across an ancient bridge, built in 1535 by Margaret Tudor's tailor to spite a ferryman who refused him passage, you come to **Doune**. To the south of the village (right), is its well-preserved medieval **castle**. This occupies a triangular site protected on two sides by the rivers Teith and Ardoch. It was the stronghold of the Earls of Moray and was used as a prison by Bonnie Prince Charlie.

Return through the village and, keeping on the A84, continue for another 7 miles (11km) to **Callander**, with its clean stone-built houses and its broad main street lined with shops. Keep an eye open, on entering the town, for the sign on the left, **Roman Camp Hotel** (tel: 01877-330 003, fax: 331 533). This tranquil country house hotel, a 16th-century hunting lodge a mere 100 yards/metres from the main road, is an excellent place to stop for a slap-up lunch. Alternatively, more modest refreshment can be found at **Dalgair House** on the main street.

A converted church, also on Callander's main street, now houses the **Rob Roy and Trossachs Visitor Centre** (daily except January and February weekends only; tel: 01877-330 342 for times) with an excellent multimedia show of Scotland's folk hero Rob Roy Macgregor, Scotland's answer to Robin Hood. Incidentally, the Macgregors

The Trossachs from Stirling

On Loch Katrine

are credited with inventing the word 'blackmail': owners of cattle were forced to pay them black meal to earn their protection.

From Callander the **Trossachs Trail** twists and turns west on the A821 for 9 miles (15km) along the banks of lochs **Venachar** and **Achray**. It then enters a short, narrow gorge of rocks and mounds covered with heather and deciduous trees, bog myrtle and foxgloves, which ends at **Loch Katrine**, flanked to the north by Benvane (2,685ft/818m) and to the southwest by Ben Venue (2,386ft/729m). It was this romantic area of outstanding natural beauty that fired the imagination of Sir Walter Scott, who used it as the location for both *The Lady of the Lake* and *Rob Roy*. Little could Scott have imagined the flood of tourists, including poets Dorothy and William Wordsworth, that his works would unleash.

Loch Katrine throbs with humanity but stroll along the road on the north shore (no vehicles permitted) and in minutes you are on your own. After one mile (1½km) the **Silver Strand** is reached with the view that is described in Scott's *Lady of the Lake*. From April to October the *SS Sir Walter Scott*, a dignified old steamboat, leaves from the pier at 11am (except Saturday) for a cruise lasting 1hr 45mins. Shorter cruises lasting an hour leave daily at 1.45pm and 3.15pm (tel: 01877-376 316 for details). Loch Katrine is the source of Glasgow's drinking water, one of the world's softest.

Backtrack the short distance to where the B829 takes off to the right and climbs steadily over the **Duke's Pass** (named after Rob Roy's implacable enemy, the Duke of Montrose) for 6 miles (10km) to Aberfoyle. En route, after 4½ miles (7km), be sure to turn left at the sign Achray Forest Drive and, after a few hundred yards, stop at a glorious view point. Afterwards return to the main road and to **Aberfoyle** which, like Callander, is a solid town bustling with tourists.

From here a detour of 28 miles (45km) to the northwest (no circuit is possible) is not for the faint-hearted. The narrow B829 twists and turns and, for much of the way, clings to the water's edge.

The open road

Loch Lomond is Scotland's largest loch

However, it is certainly rewarding. The road runs past **Loch Ard** and **Loch Chon** before coming to a T-junction. First, take the short drive of about one mile (1½km) to the right which will bring you to **Stronachlachar**, a peaceful spot at the western end of Loch Katrine with the most glorious of views. A left at the T takes you downhill for 4 miles (6km) to **Inversnaid** and its waterfall on the banks of **Loch Lomond**. This is one of the most advantageous spots from which to view Scotland's largest, most visited and most celebrated loch. It is also a good opportunity to stop for afternoon tea at the **Inversnaid Hotel** (tel: 01877-386 223).

Back at Aberfoyle proceed west and, at the end of the town, turn right for 8 miles (13km) on the A811 to **Drymen**, a road that passes through pleasant agricultural land. Drymen has a charming village green and, if you failed to have tea at Inversnaid, would be an ideal place to stop. From Drymen continue on the B837 through **Buchanan**, along a small country road with good views across the loch and on to **Balmaha**, 6 miles (10km) from Drymen. Balmaha is a major boating centre on Loch Lomond.

Return to Drymen and continue on the A811 for 10 miles (16km) until Arnprior where a left onto the B8034 leads, after 5 miles (8km), to Port of Menteith and placid **Lake of Menteith** (the only inland body of water in Scotland designated 'lake' rather than 'loch'). From here ferries make the 10-minute journey (April to September) to the island of **Inchmahome** with its simple, well-preserved 13th-century priory set among majestic sycamores and oaks. Here Robert the Bruce prayed before his epic victory at Bannockburn and young Mary Queen of Scots played beneath the great walls of the priory. In rare hard winters the lake freezes over and the Grand Match is staged, when hundreds take to the ice for a day's curling.

Continue eastwards on the A873. South of the village of Thornhill is **Flanders Moss**, a National Nature Reserve and a remnant of the ancient raised peat bog which once covered much of the Forth Valley. Stirling Castle now comes back into view and you are soon on the A84 and then the M9 back to Edinburgh.

Option 1. Edinburgh: Sights, Arts and Shops

A morning's sightseeing on Calton Hill followed by a stroll along Princes Street and visits to art galleries.

– To the start: Calton Hill, immediately beyond the east end of Princes Street, is easily reached by steps from Regent Road which is well served by bus. Alternatively drive to the car park at the summit of the hill. The route for this itinerary is contained on the map of Edinburgh on page 22 –

Calton Hill was left undeveloped when the New Town was being built, but in 1776 James Craig constructed an observatory here, replaced in 1818 by William Playfair's former observatory presently on the site. But by far the most striking structure on the hill is Playfair's and Cockerell's 12-columned portico – the **National Monument** commemorating those who died in the Napoleonic Wars. Intended as a replica of the Parthenon, which is dedicated rather ironically to Athena, Goddess of War, construction of this monument nicknamed 'Edinburgh's Disgrace' or 'Scotland's Pride and Poverty' was stopped because of a lack of funds.

The National Monument imitates the Parthenon

The Scott Monument

The views of Edinburgh and its surroundings from the hill are superb, but they are even better if you have the energy to climb the 143 steps of the 106-ft (32-m) high **Nelson Monument** erected in 1815 (April to September, Monday 1–6pm, Tuesday to Saturday 10am–6pm; October to March, Monday to Saturday 10am–3pm; tel: 0131-556 2716). The monument at the western end of the hill honours Dugald Stewart, Professor of Moral Philosophy at Edinburgh University. At the southeast corner is a Playfair monument to his uncle, the mathematician and natural philosopher, John Playfair.

Descend from the hill to Regent Road and walk westwards for a few hundred yards to the busy intersection of Waterloo Place and Leith Street. Across the road is the massive frontage of the **General Register House** from the drawing board of Robert Adam, the great 18th-century Scottish architect. Now cross the road to the street level of the **Waverley Shopping Centre** where **Café Vienna** serves coffee.

You are now on **Princes Street**, whose east end is dominated by the **Scott Monument** (June to September: Monday to Saturday 9am to 8pm or dusk if earlier, Sunday 10am–6pm; March to May and October: daily 10am–6pm; rest of the year: daily 10am–4pm; tel: 0131-529 4068). This Edinburgh landmark, now reopened with displays inside after years enclosed in scaffolding, is a 200-ft (61-m) high elaborate neo-Gothic steeple which acts as a canopy for a statue of Sir Walter Scott. Characters from his writings and the heads of 16 Scottish poets adorn the monument. To see inside or reach the upper terrace with views, you must negotiate a narrow spiral staircase.

Further west, on the same side of Princes Street, are two neoclassical buildings, one behind the other, from the drawing board of William Playfair. Visit the rear building, the **National Gallery of Scotland** (Monday to Saturday 10am–5pm, Sunday 2–5pm; tel: 0131-624 6220) and enjoy an exquisite, yet not overwhelming, collection of Old Masters, Impressionists and Scottish painters. The front building belongs to the **Royal Scottish Academy** which mounts an annual

On Princes Street

exhibition of members' art in spring/summer (tel: 0131-225 6671 for details of this and other exhibitions). The hill immediately west of the two buildings is **The Mound** linking the New and Old Town – made with earth taken from the New Town building site.

Descend the steps into the renowned **Princes Street Gardens** and walk through the gardens, overlooked all the time by the Castle. Modern art lovers may wish to continue until the exit at St John's church, then cross Princes Street and walk up to parallel **George Street** in order to board the No 13 (red) bus for a 5-minute journey to the **Scottish National Gallery of Modern Art** and the **Dean Gallery** on Belford Road (both galleries: Monday to Saturday 10am–5pm, Sunday 2–5pm; extended hours during the Festival; free except special exhibitions; tel: 0131-624 6220). The main, national gallery has works by Braque, Picasso, Matisse, Magritte, Hockney and others, and also houses a collection of recent Scottish work; figures by Henry Moore and others lounge on the lawn. The new Dean Gallery contains Dada and Surrealist works. You could do worse than lunch in the main museum's licensed restaurant, which has an outdoor terrace.

Alternatively, walk up the Mound to the High Street and ahead along George IV Bridge to lunch in **Elephant House**, a popular coffee house at No. 21 on the right, before turning into Chambers Street for the new **Museum of Scotland** (tel: 0131-247 4422) and, linked to it, the Victorian **Royal Museum** (tel: 0131-225 7534). The former brings together important relics from Scotland's history whereas the latter contains globally-sourced displays on science, natural history and history. (Both open Monday to Saturday 10am–5pm, Tuesday till 8pm, Sunday noon–5pm.)

Henry Moore in Edinburgh

Those who want to stay and shop in Princes Street, and who would like a simple lunch with a view of the castle, can make for self-service restaurants in **Debenhams** at the street's west end or **Jenners** further east.

Option 2. Edinburgh's New Town

An afternoon stroll through the New Town where building commenced in the mid-18th century, when overcrowding became severe in the Old Town. See the magnificent architecture of Charlotte Square and Moray Place. Visits to museums.

– To the start: innumerable buses stop in or near St Andrew Square. The route for this itinerary is on the map of Edinburgh on page 22 –

The saving graces of **St Andrew Square** are the two magnificent banks standing on its eastern side. The **Royal Bank of Scotland**, fronted by a garden in which stands an equestrian statue of the Earl of Hopetoun, was once a splendid Georgian town house. Its sumptuous yet simple banking hall, whose glorious dome is pierced by 120 stars, was added in 1860. Next door, not to be outdone by its rival, is the **Bank of Scotland** with its handsome telling room featuring six bold Corinthian columns that are topped by statues representing navigation, commerce, manufacturing, science, art and agriculture. On the friezes are a dozen medallions of eminent Scots including Adam Smith, James Watt and Walter Scott.

Bank of Scotland, St Andrew Square

Exit from the west side of the square into **George Street**, designed as the principal street of the first New Town. Immediately on your right, fronted by a portico, is the oval **Church of St Andrew and St George**. The Disruption which led to the formation of the Free Church of Scotland was led from here in 1843 by Dr Chalmers. In case you are unaware of the history of banking in this area I should point out the former Royal Bank of Scotland building across the road. Possibly in an attempt to show who is the more powerful, God or Mammon, its portico boasts six fluted Corinthian columns as opposed to the four plain columns of the church. It now houses the Dome café-bar and nightclub.

Somewhat further along, past the intersection with Hanover Street where stands an equestrian statue of George IV, are the **Assembly Rooms**, a two-storey classical building with a three-arched arcade projecting onto the pavement, once the social focus for the New Town and much used by 19th-century musicians and entertainers (including Chopin and Dickens). It was here that Sir Walter Scott publically admitted his authorship of the *Waverley Novels* (in those

On George Street

days it wasn't the done thing for an aristocrat to be a writer). During the Festival this is a major Fringe venue and ceilidhs are held here throughout the year (tel: 0131-220 4348).

Continue to the western end of George Street and then veer left to pass round the south side of **Charlotte Square** which features some of the most splendid Georgian architecture in Europe. On the west side of the square, **St George's Church** with its green dome provides the focal point for George Street. It is now an annexe of the Scottish Records Office.

Turning into the north side you are faced by the dignified facade of Robert Adam's masterpiece of urban architecture. At No. 7, the **Georgian House** (April to October: Monday to Saturday 10am–5pm; Sunday 2–5pm; tel: 0131-226 3318), you can experience the gracious lifestyle of a wealthy family in 1796. Three floors here are furnished as they would have been during the reign of George III. Next door, No. 6, is the official home of the Secretary of State for Scotland. A new museum close by may be open by now, dedicated to the inventor of the telephone, Alexander Graham Bell. If you wish to visit the Bell Museum in the house in which the inventor was born, at 16 South Charlotte Street, turn left out of the Georgian House, then right and ahead a short distance.

Return to the square. Those who would like to savour more of the architectural harmony of the New Town should make for its north-west corner and take short Glenfinlas Street, which leads you to Ainslie Place. Turn right here and exit on short Great Stuart Street which leads into magnificent 12-sided **Moray Place** where Tuscan porticos lord it over private gardens. This, in my opinion, is the gem of the New Town. Stroll around in a clockwise direction and exit on Forres Street which leads into Queen Street. Turn left here. Alternatively, return to George Street and immediately turn left into Castle Street where No. 39, with distinctive shallow bow windows, was the home of Sir Walter Scott from 1802–26. Continue to the crossroads and turn right.

Broad, busy Queen Street, parallel to George Street, has private buildings (mainly offices) on the left and gardens on the right which are unfortunately exclusively for the use of the occupants of these buildings (you need a key to get in). When you reach Hanover Street, a few steps up on the left you will find No. 121 and the basement **Laigh Bake House** (tel: 0131-225 1552) a tiny, very Scottish, very traditional tearoom whose hazelnut cake and cheese scones are simply magic.

Original furnishings in the Georgian House

Back on Queen Street you soon come across the distinctive Victorian gothic **Scottish National Portrait Gallery** (Monday to Saturday 10am–5pm, Sunday 2–5pm; tel: 0131-624 6200; free except special exhibitions), with paintings, photographs and busts of famous Scots (and a few non Scots) from Mary Queen of Scots to the Queen Mother and Muriel Spark, and Sir Walter Scott to Winston Churchill.

Option 3. Edinburgh's Pubs

An evening tour of some of the New Town's best public houses, concentrated in and around one street.

Few, if any, will be capable of stopping at all the pubs on this safari, for to do so would mean the ability to consume 15 pints. I suggest a start at the **Guildford Arms**, on West Register Street (just behind the east end of Princes Street), a beautiful ornate pub from the end of the last century with stained wood, mirrors and a lofty ribbed ceiling which permits a gallery bar. Practically next door at the better known and more expensive **Café Royal Circle Bar,** which first opened its doors in 1862, is more of the same plus a vast selection of malt whiskies. At this point you might wish to fortify yourself at the café's renowned Oyster Bar.

Books and beer at Finlays

Milne's has aspirations

Continue along West Register Street to south St Andrew's Street and turn left to immediately descend a few steps into **Finlays** which outsmarts many of the pubs that carry daily newspapers by having a well-thumbed library of undistinguished books. Cross the road and cut through Meuse Lane to South St David Street, then cross over again to enter pedestrianised Rose Street.

Your first stop on Rose Street should be the **Abbotsford**, redolent with Victorian charm and with a good restaurant (a cut above pub grub; tel: 0131-225 5276) upstairs. Next comes **Milne's**, an old pub with a recent extension making it one of the largest venues on this route. It is often frequented by those with literary aspirations.

Cross Hanover Street, leaving the **Three Tuns** on the left and pass the small **Thirty-Seven Bar**, which has a splendid gantry, and **Paddy's Bar**. Next comes the **Rose Street Brewery** which was still brewing on the pub premises until very recently; upstairs is a steak-house. Then comes the **Auld Hundred**, a small bar with a busy upstairs restaurant serving good inexpensive pub grub. Almost opposite is the back entrance to **The Standing Order**. This is a grand and cavernous former bank (fronting on George Street) with a high, ornate ceiling, an old safe still in one of the side rooms and lessons in Scottish history beside portraits of famous Scots on the walls.

The Kenilworth

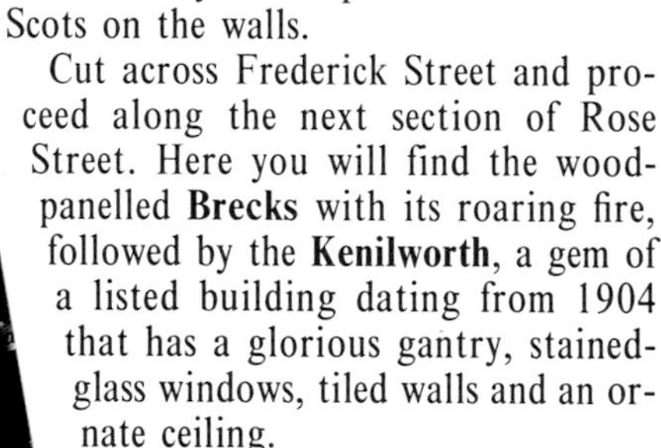

Cut across Frederick Street and proceed along the next section of Rose Street. Here you will find the wood-panelled **Brecks** with its roaring fire, followed by the **Kenilworth**, a gem of a listed building dating from 1904 that has a glorious gantry, stained-glass windows, tiled walls and an ornate ceiling.

Pubs come with a rush in the final block of this street: among them are the **Rose and Crown**, the **Gordon Arms**, and the Georgian **Scott's Bar** which features low ceilings, Tiffany lamps and fresh flowers on the table. Scott's is a good place to collapse in a refined atmosphere before you return to your hotel.

Option 4. Two Towns

A morning visit to Culross, the best-preserved 16th/17th-century town in Scotland, and to Dunfermline, the one-time capital.

– To the start: leave Edinburgh by the A90 (Forth Road Bridge) and turn onto the road marked Rosyth, where the A985 is joined. This leads after 4 miles (7km) to a roundabout with Culross signposted to the left. The route for this itinerary is on the map below –

Driving into this once bustling port is like travelling backwards in time. Since 1931, the Royal Burgh of **Culross** (pronounced *cooruss*) has been preserved by the National Trust for Scotland as a perfect example of a small Scottish burgh of the 16th and 17th centuries. The entire village is a historical monument whose character can be readily explored in a steep uphill walk through the narrow cobbled streets and wynds to end up at Culross Abbey.

After morning coffee at the **Red Lion** start your visit at the **Town House** or **Tolbooth** which was built in 1626 with the addition of the clock tower and a new frontage in 1783. Here you can watch a short audiovisual presentation which informs you that the wealth of the town came from coal mining, salt panning and a monopoly on the manufacture of iron girdles for baking. Also in the Town House are the prison,

The Tolbooth, Culross

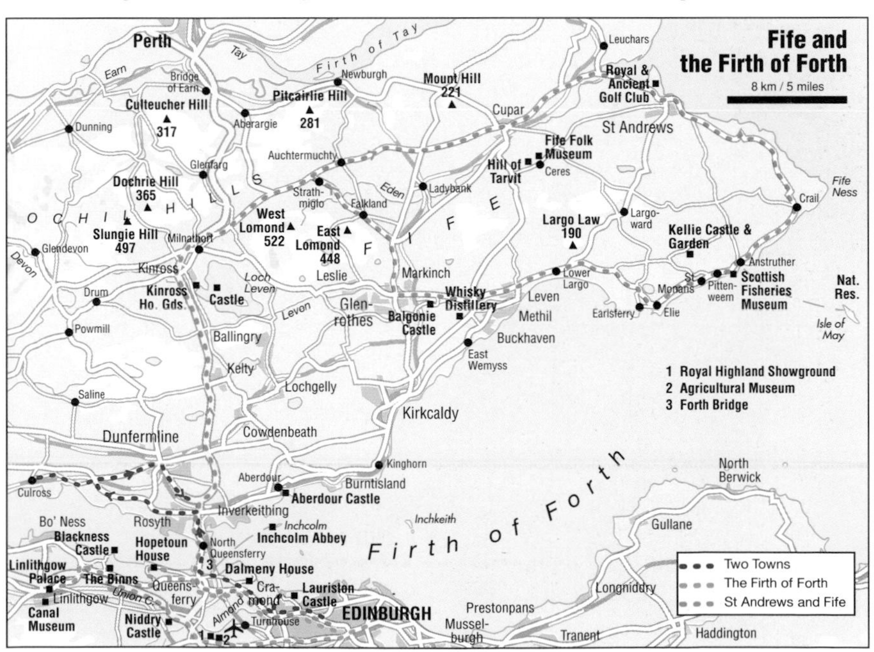

The Palace

the courtroom and the debtors' room (April to September: daily 1–5pm, July and August from 10am; October: weekends only, 1–5pm; tel: 01383-880 359; tickets include entry to Palace and Study – *see below*).

Nearby is the magnificent yellow-coloured **Palace** (open as Town House), the grandest house in the village and *the* place in Scotland to see how prosperous 17th-century merchants lived. It was built in several stages at the start of the 17th century by Sir George Bruce, the richest and most famous citizen of Culross. Baltic timber and Dutch tiles which decorate the Palace are testimony to trade with Holland. Outstanding is the Allegory Ceiling, which has 16 scenes, each with a motto, painted on the pine barrel-vaulting. The delightful terraced garden behind the Palace should be visited.

Explore the town by taking a stroll along the **Back Causeway** which debouches into a tiny atmospheric square whose centrepiece is a copy of the original 1588 **Mercat Cross**. In the square you should visit the **Study** (open as Town House), which owes its name to the room at the top of the corbelled projecting tower. The main room has a restored 17th-century painted ceiling and original 1633 panelling. Continue the climb on cobbled streets past white-harled houses with rust-coloured pantiled roofs, carved lintels, inscribed panels and arms of guilds and craftsmen. One of these, on the right, is the **Snuffmakers House** which bears the inscription 'Who would have thocht it'. The second part of the rhyme, 'noses have bocht it' is on a house in Edinburgh.

At the top of the steep hill – your climb will be rewarded by grand views of the Firth of Forth – is the **Cistercian Abbey** of which little remains. Founded in 1217, the abbey has some similarities to Inchcolm (*see Option 7*). The central tower and choir have been incorporated into the adjoining parish church.

Once you've seen enough, backtrack from Culross on the B937 and at the roundabout take the A994 which after 3 miles (5km) enters **Dunfermline**. Lest you forget that Scotland's capital for six centuries is the burial place of one of the country's great heroes, the words 'King Robert the Bruce' are carved out on the balustrade of

Dunfermline

the parish church tower. The church stands alongside extensive ruins of a Benedictine **Abbey**, founded by Queen Margaret in the 11th century, and a **Palace**. (Both abbey and palace are open April to September: daily 9.30am–6.30pm; October to March: Monday to Wednesday and Saturday 9.30am–4.30pm, Thursday 9.30am–12.30pm, Sunday 2–4.30pm; tel: 01383-739 026).

On Moodie Street, a few hundred yards southeast of the Abbey, stands the birthplace of Andrew Carnegie, now the **Andrew Carnegie Museum** (April to September: Monday to Saturday 11am–5pm, Sunday 2–5pm; tel: 01383-724 302). Carnegie emigrated to the US and became a steel magnate and great philanthropist, remembered by New York's Carnegie Hall. The first of nearly 3,000 Carnegie libraries was established in Dunfermline in 1881.

Leave Dunfermline for Edinburgh (17 miles/28km) on the A907 which immediately leads to the M90 and the Forth Bridge.

Option 5. Crieff, Crafts and Whisky

A morning drive into the Highlands with a visit to a distillery and the opportunity to watch artisans at work.

– To the start: leave the west end of Edinburgh on the A90 (Queensferry Road) and after crossing the Forth Bridge continue on the M90 to Perth (42 miles/67km) –

At the northern edge of Perth, just off the Inveralmond roundabout on the A9, you can get a taste of things to come at **Caithness Glass** (large shop opens at 9am Monday to Saturday, 10am Sunday; watch glass-making in the factory weekdays 9am–4.30pm; tel: 01738-637 373). You'll see more coloured glass at Perthshire Paperweights, so you may wish to forego the stop in Perth and go straight to Crieff, due west 17 miles (27km) on the A85.

Crieff, overlooking the River Earn, exudes an air of prosperity which it owes to Victorian days when it was a popular spa. The stocks outside the Town Hall suggest it was not always so. Continue past the town for half-a-mile to visit the clearly signposted **Glenturret Distillery**, which was established in 1775 and claims to be Scotland's oldest. Guided tours are held all day (Sunday from noon) and the

Copper stills for whisky

Making glass

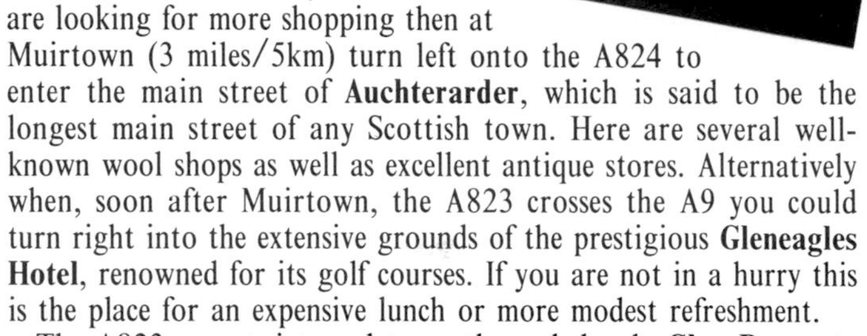

Visitor Centre has a good restaurant and coffee shop.

Leave Crieff to the south on the A822 and stop at the **Visitor Centre** to see hand-painted ware with Scottish motifs produced in **Buchan's Thistle Pottery**, the oldest in the country, and the making of millefiori glass at **Perthshire Paperweights**. (both open only on working days; tel: 01764-654 014.) Across the road you can visit the **Stuart Crystal Factory Shop**.

Continue on the A822 until just beyond Muthill (3 miles/5km) where you turn left onto the A823. If you are looking for more shopping then at Muirtown (3 miles/5km) turn left onto the A824 to enter the main street of **Auchterarder**, which is said to be the longest main street of any Scottish town. Here are several well-known wool shops as well as excellent antique stores. Alternatively when, soon after Muirtown, the A823 crosses the A9 you could turn right into the extensive grounds of the prestigious **Gleneagles Hotel**, renowned for its golf courses. If you are not in a hurry this is the place for an expensive lunch or more modest refreshment.

The A823 now twists and turns through lovely **Glen Devon** to arrive after 10 miles (16km) at **Rumbling Bridge**. Park in what appears to be the parking lot of a nursing home and walk down the path to view the river tumbling through a ravine.

Return to Edinburgh via the A823, the B914 where a left turn leads to the M90 motorway and a straight run to the capital.

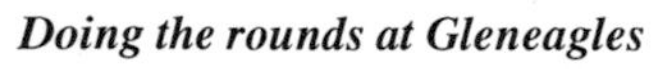

Doing the rounds at Gleneagles

Option 6. The Firth of Forth

An afternoon visiting stately homes on the Firth of Forth and a ruined but distinguished palace.

– To the start: leave the west end of Edinburgh on the A90 (Queensferry Road) and after 8 miles (13km) turn off onto the A904 and follow the signs to Hopetoun House, a further 2 miles (3km). *See map on page 45 –*

Hopetoun House (Easter to September: daily 10am–5.30pm; October: weekends 10am–5.30pm; tel: 0131-331 2451) is a splendid massive pile with extravagant interiors set in extensive parkland. Sir William Bruce was the architect of the original house which dates to the start of the 18th century. William Adam enlarged this and his work was continued by his sons, Robert and James, who were especially involved in the interior decoration of the State Apartments.

The collection of paintings here includes Titians, Canalettos and works by Rubens as well as portraits by Gainsborough and Ramsay. If you hire the dining room, which has retained all its Regency decoration and furnishings, including the Derby dessert service and wine coolers for very special functions, you might wish to try to emulate George IV, who lunched here on turtle soup and three glasses of wine. Noteworthy in the ballroom are 17th-century French tapestries illustrating scenes from Virgil's *Aeneid*. Extensive and immaculate grounds are home to red and fallow deer and rare four-horned black St Kilda sheep, and offer magnificent views (which are even better from the rooftop observatory) of the two Forth bridges. Before leaving visit the snack bar or licensed restaurant in the Tapestry Room.

Hopetoun's sumptuous interior

Exit from Hopetoun House by driving through the walled garden and then turning right and, after 1½ miles (2km) on an unclassified road, reaching the main road (A904). Turn right here and after 2 miles (3km) arrive at **The House of The Binns** (May to September: daily except Friday 1.30–5.30pm; tel: 01506-834 255). The exterior of this house, which represents an early 17th-century transitional stage from fortress to gracious mansion, is intriguing as are the tall tales told about Tam Dalyell, the house's most notorious owner (ancestor of the present politician with the same name). Superb panoramas can be enjoyed from the base of a ruined tower in the grounds.

St Michael, Linlithgow

Continue on the A904 and turn left after 1 mile (2km) onto the A803 which leads after 2½ miles (4km) to the town of **Linlithgow** where signs indicate the **Palace** (April to September: daily 9.30am–6.30pm; rest of the year: 9.30am–4.30pm; tel: 01506-842 896), a glorious roofless red sandstone shell atop a mound above the eponymous loch. Mary Queen of Scots was born in this mainly 15th-century palace whilst her father James V lay dying at Falkland Palace. The adjacent **Church of St Michael** is contemporary with the Palace and is the largest pre-Reformation church to survive in Scotland. Here James IV saw the ghost which warned him of defeat at Flodden Field.

On leaving the Palace backtrack for 2 miles (3km) on the A803 to reach the M9 motorway. Edinburgh is 17 miles (32km) away.

Option 7. Inchcolm

An afternoon trip to Inchcolm island and its abbey.

– To the start: leave the west end of Edinburgh on the A90 (Queensferry Road) and, after 8 miles (13km) take the B924 which immediately arrives at Queensferry (free parking at Hawes Pier) –

'Maid of the Forth' and the Forth Rail Bridge

From Easter to October the *Maid of the Forth* usually sails at 12.30pm, 2pm and/or 3pm, although this can vary depending on the month. School sailings depart at 10.15am and 11.45am on most weekdays in June and have space for adults (tel: 0131-331 4857 for details and bookings). The excursion takes 2½ hours.

Historically, and until the Forth Road Bridge was built in 1964, **South Queensferry** (invariably called **Queensferry**) was

Calm sunshine on the rivermouth at Cramond

the site of a ferry which carried pilgrims across the Forth for the short journey to Dunfermline Abbey. Overshadowed by its modern bridges, the old village is still worth a stroll. **Hawes Inn** (1633) is where David Balfour in Robert Louis Stevenson's *Kidnapped* was lured aboard the brig *Covenanter.*

The *Maid* first sails under the railway bridge and after about 45 minutes – seals are often seen en route – arrives at the tiny island of **Inchcolm**, the Iona of the East, which is renowned because of **Inchcolm Abbey** (tel: 0131-331 4857). The original building was a thank-you from Alexander I who was stormbound on the island in 1123 and received hospitality from a hermit monk. On landing, stroll in the pleasant gardens and visit the 13th–15th century ruins which include cloisters and an unusual octagonal chapter house. Shakespeare mentions the island in *Macbeth* as the burial place of the defeated Sweno of Norway and a hog-backed gravestone may date from this period.

Return to Edinburgh on the B924 and A90 but on reaching the busy Barnton roundabout (about 4 miles/6km from Queensferry) turn left onto Whitehouse Road into the tiny village of **Cramond** at the mouth of the River Almond. The picturesque **Cramond Inn** is in the centre of this lovely village of whitewashed 18th-century houses. A short stroll away in the parish churchyard are the ruins of Roman fortifications. And so back to Edinburgh.

Tea in the open

1. A Day in the Borders

A visit to the Borders with glorious vistas of the River Tweed, visits to abbeys and stately homes and lots of opportunities to shop for tweeds.

– To the start: leave Edinburgh on the A703 and drive 23 miles (37km) south to the bustling town of Peebles –

In **Peebles** stroll along the High Street, which has some interesting old-fashioned stores. Then proceed to the **Sunflower** (4 Bridgegate), a renowned tiny specialist food shop and restaurant where you can enjoy a cup of coffee. If this is not yet open then upstairs at the **Country Shop** (43 High Street) is a good alternative.

Leave Peebles by the bridge over the **River Tweed** where you may see salmon fishermen standing in the shallows. Immediately turn left and continue along the south bank of the river (B7062) for 6 miles (10km) to **Traquair House**, said to be the oldest continually inhabited house in Scotland. (April, May and September from 12.30pm; June to August from 10.30am; October from 12.30pm Friday and Saturday only; closes 5.30pm; tel: 01896-830 323.)

The Maxwell-Stuarts, the owners of Traquair, supported the

Welcome to Peebles

Stuarts and when Bonnie Prince Charlie was defeated they closed the gates of their home and vowed not to open them until the Stuarts regained the throne. The 'Bear Gates' are still closed but there is another entrance to the house. With almost 1,000 years of history behind it and visits from 27 monarchs, Traquair has plenty to offer the visitor, including a maze and an excellent strong ale that is made by the family and sold from an 18th-century brewhouse.

On leaving Traquair, turn left and then left again to cross the Tweed river. Next turn right onto the A72. The views of the river here are quite beautiful. Con-

Stone noble, Dryburgh

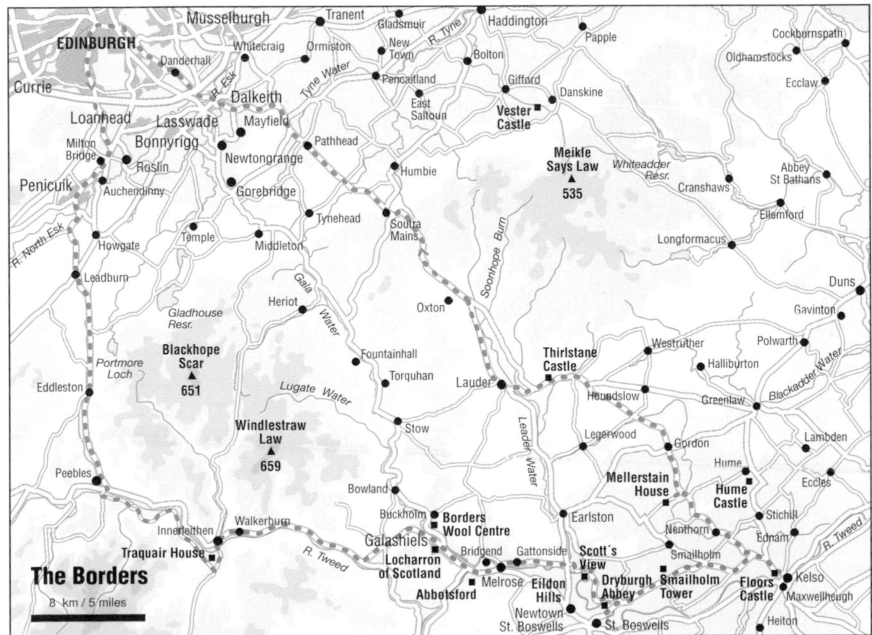

Pipe band, Traquair

trary to popular belief, the word 'tweed' does not owe its origins to the river. It resulted, rather more strangely, from an English clerk working in London in 1829 who misread the word *tweels*, a Scottish word for cloth. The road passes through Walkerburn after 2 miles (4km) and continues for a further 12 miles (20km) to **Galashiels** which, since the Industrial Revolution, has been the centre of the Scottish woollen weaving industry.

Galashiels' one-way streets present something of a problem to the stranger but be single-minded and you will arrive at Huddersfield Street and **Lochcarron of Scotland Cashmere and Wool Centre** (tel: 01896-752 091). Here you can enjoy a historical display about the woollen industry, 40-minute tours of the modern mill (Monday to Thursday at 10.30am, 11.30am, 1.30pm and 2.30pm; Friday at 10.30 and 11.30am), a demonstration of spinning and a cornucopia of woollens for sale in the shop, including 754 different tartans The shop and museum open Monday to Saturday 9am–5pm, plus June to September: Sunday noon–5pm.

Dryburgh Abbey

Lovers of abbeys or teddy bears should, before proceeding to Gattonside, continue straight through the roundabout for 1 mile (2km) to the town of **Melrose** with its glorious ruined Abbey (open daily; tel: 01896-822 562), which contains the heart of Robert the Bruce. The Border Abbeys were destroyed in the mid-16th century by Henry VIII's troops during the invasion known as the 'Rough Wooing'. Melrose, started here in the 12th century, was a Cistercian foundation. Nearby in the High Street is the **Teddy Melrose Museum and Bear Shop** (summer: Monday to Saturday 9am–5pm, Sunday noon–5pm; winter: weekends; tel: 01896-823 854) where you can discover everything you ever wanted to know about teddies.

From Galashiels, drive up the short hill (Hill Street) opposite the exit to Lochcarron and turn left onto the main road (A7). After 2 miles (4km) exit from the second roundabout and drive for ½ mile (800m) to **Abbotsford** (late March to October: Monday to Saturday 10am–5pm, Sunday 2–5pm, June to September from 10am on Sunday; tel: 01896-752 043), the last home of Sir Walter Scott and one which he designed himself. Scott's magnificent study containing about 9,000 rare books has been preserved as he left it and the house also contains a comprehensive collection of historic weapons. His love of curiosities is evident in an extensive collection of paraphernalia which includes Prince Charlie's *quaich* (drinking bowl) and Rob Roy's gun. After viewing the house stroll through the gardens and view the private chapel added after Scott's death.

Your next goal is **Scott's View** which is reached by returning to the large roundabout and continuing for 1 mile (2km) to the next roundabout. Leave this by the Gattonside exit (B6360) to the left which immediately crosses over a single-lane bridge, after which you should turn right and drive for 4 miles (6km) passing under a magnificent viaduct, and pick up the sign 'Scott's View'.

It was from atop **Bemersyde Hill** (593ft/180m) that Scott enjoyed the delightful view which encompasses the triple Eildon Hills on the far side of the Tweed. From here proceed downhill for a couple of miles to a T-junction: turn right and immediately reach **Dryburgh Abbey** (open daily; tel: 01835-822 381). Scott is buried in this tranquil ruin set in the most beautiful grounds through which the River Tweed flows. The **Dryburgh Abbey Hotel**, next to the ruin, is a pleasant, reasonably-priced and comfortable place for sandwiches or a more formal lunch (tel: 01835-822 261).

You should next turn back and drive along the B6356 for 10 miles (16km) through rolling cultivated hills to a T-junction with the A6089. Turn right and, passing the back of Floors Castle, the property of the Duke of Roxburghe, you almost immediately arrive at **Kelso** with its lovely, somewhat French cobbled town

Kelso Abbey

The Duke of Roxburghe in Floors Castle

square and a rather smart – if traditional – local population. Just west of the square are the ruins of **Kelso Abbey** (daily; free). Scanty though these are, this was once the largest and grandest of the Border abbeys. Scott attended a grammar school held in the abbey's aisle.

On the outskirts of Kelso stands **Floors Castle** (Easter weekend to October: daily 10am–4.30pm; tel: 01573-223 333), the property of the Duke of Roxburghe and the largest private residence in Scotland. You must make a decision at this point. Should you visit Floors, the work of William Adam, patriarch of a distinguished family of Scottish architects, and later embellished with a forest of domes, spires and turrets by William Playfair? (Floors' major attractions in those few rooms open to the public are fine tapestries, a small collection of post-Impressionist paintings and some Chinese porcelains.) Or should you opt for Mellerstain on the road back to Edinburgh? I prefer the latter: both have pleasant tearooms.

Whereas Floors is set in lovely grounds through which the River Tweed flows, the Georgian house **Mellerstain** has beautiful gardens, a sumptuous interior and a collection of paintings (Gainsborough, Constable and others) that have earned it the accolade of 'the most beautiful Adam house in Scotland'. Although William started to build Mellerstain, it is his son Robert, 'an architect of genius', who was responsible for its glorious interiors. Opening hours at Mellerstain are Easter weekend and May to September: Sunday to Friday 12.30–5pm; tel: 01573-410 225. It is reached by leaving Kelso and travelling north on the A6089 through gently rising pastoral country for 8 miles (13km).

After the visit continue through the same delightful countryside to Gordon and take a short detour through attractive Lauder on the A68. Stay on this road all the way back to Edinburgh, a total of 56 miles (90km) from Kelso.

2. St Andrews and Fife

A day trip to Fife, referred to as the Kingdom, visiting St Andrews, seaside villages and historical castles.

– To the start (St Andrews): leave the west end of Edinburgh on the the A90 (Queensferry Road) which, after 8 miles (13km), leads to the Forth Bridge (toll). Cross the bridge and continue on the M90 motorway for 13 miles (21km) to junction 8 (Milnathort exit). Join the A91 marked Cupar and St Andrews, a further 23 miles (37km). See maps on page 45 and below –

Those golfers whose main interest at St Andrews is the **Old Course** will have booked a start time months before leaving home. But two-thirds of all start times in a day are allocated by ballot the day before. To be included, contact the starter (tel: 01334-466 666) before 2pm on the day before you wish to play (closed Sunday). Handicap certificates (28 for men, 36 for women) or a letter of introduction are required. Many consider the New Course (for which booking is not mandatory) more challenging than the Old.

Clubhouse, St Andrews

If you plan to eat at **The Cellar** in Anstruther, which serves superb seafood lunches (currently Wednesday to Saturday only), you should book before setting out on this itinerary (24 East Green; tel: 01333-310 378).

Anyone interested in Mary Queen of Scots might wish to make a 75-minute excursion on leaving the motorway at Milnathort.

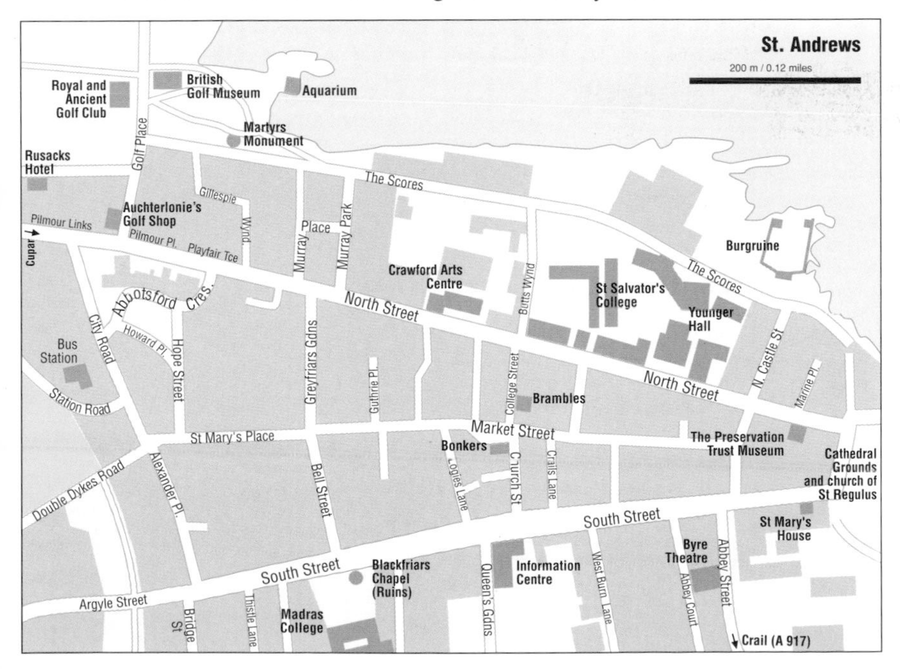

Cathedral ruins

Rather than joining the A91, turn right onto the B936. This passes through Milnathort and then immediately enters Kinross where a narrow, signposted road to the left leads to Loch Leven and a jetty from where ferries leave on a 20-minute voyage to Castle Island (April to September: daily 9.30am–6.30pm; tel: 0378-040 483). Mary was held prisoner here in **Loch Leven Castle** in 1567, before escaping with the aid of 16-year-old Willy Douglas. Willy locked everyone in the castle and threw the keys in the loch. Thirteen days later Mary was defeated at the Battle of Langside.

Back on the A91 en route to St Andrews observe the twin Lomond Hills (no relation to Loch Lomond) on the right and, especially after Cupar, the glorious agricultural landscape on the left. Those interested in an unsurpassed selection of whisky may want to stop at **Luvians Bottle Shop** (also good wines) which is on the left as you pass through Cupar (93 Bonnygate; tel: 01334-654 820).

Immediately on entering **St Andrews** the Old Course is to the left. Stop for morning coffee at the reasonably-priced **Rusacks Hotel** whose elegant Victorian lounge overlooks the 18th green and 1st tee of the Old. Alternatively, you can enjoy inexpensive snacks at **Brambles** (5 College Street) in the heart of town.

You don't need to golf to enjoy a round on the putting green attached to the Old Course or a visit to the excellent **British Golf Museum** (Easter to mid-October: 9.30am–5.30pm; rest of the year: Thursday to Monday 11am–3pm; tel: 01334-478 880) which is very much a hands-on, state-of-the-art museum, immediately across the road from the clubhouse.

But St Andrews is much more than just golf. It is Scotland's old ecclesiastical capital and was in the thick of Scottish history. Its rich heritage includes a **Castle**, Cathedral and University. The first of these stands 400 yds

Cottages in Crail

Fresh crab at Crail

(366m) east of the links on a rock overlooking the North Sea. From it John Knox, who studied and preached in St Andrews, was captured by the French and transported to France. The castle (April to September: daily 9.30am–6.30pm; October to March: Monday to Saturday 9.30am–4.30pm, Sunday 2–4.30pm; tel: 01334-477 196) has a superb bottle dungeon.

Just beyond the castle are the outstanding and upstanding remains of the **Cathedral** (open as Castle; joint ticket available; tel: 01334-472 568), the largest religious building ever constructed in Scotland. Here, much of the drama of the Scottish Reformation was enacted. Tradition has it that in 345 the Greek monk Regulus landed here with the relics of St Andrew who became the patron saint of Scotland. For glorious views climb the tower (151 steps) of the adjacent **Church of St Regulus**, which pre-dates the cathedral and may have been built to shelter St Andrew's relics.

All around are signs of Scotland's oldest university (organised tours twice daily from July to September) whose founding in 1412 was prompted by the quest for religious knowledge. The initials PH in the cobbles in front of the gates of **St Salvator's College** on North Street, the oldest part of the University, mark where Patrick Hamilton, the first martyr of the Reformation, was burnt in 1528. His death achieved the opposite of what was intended for it is said 'the reek of Patrick Hamilton infected all it blew on'. From here stroll up short College Street to Market Street where a St Andrew's cross in the cobbles marks where the Bohemian Paul Crawer was burnt for heresy in 1433 and Pierre de Chatelard, a French gallant obsessed with Mary Queen of Scots, was executed. Chatelard's last words were: 'Adieu the most beautiful and most cruel princess of the world.'

Sightseeing concluded, you might wish to shop. Near the golf course is **Auchterlonie's**, a must for golfers. In town **Bonkers**, at the corner of Church and Market Streets, is ideal for gifts. If you are not too hungry already and are in the mood for a truly gourmet, yet not that expensive, seafood lunch then I recommend waiting till you get to Anstruther for **The Cellar** (see *page 57*).

Leave St Andrews on the A917 and after 12 miles (20km) you will reach **Crail**, the first and many say the most beautiful of the half-dozen delightful fishing villages that constitute the East Neuk of Fife. These villages were once actively trading with the Hanseatic League and the Low Countries and were King James VI's 'fringe of gold'. On the way to Crail visit **Scotland's Nuclear Bunker** (Easter to October daily 10am–5pm; tel: 01333-310 301), an amazing underground complex intended for use after a nuclear war. Four miles

Mending fishing nets at Pittenweem

(7km) beyond Crail is busy **Anstruther**, popular with day trippers, which has the outstanding **Scottish Fisheries Museum** (April to October: Monday to Saturday 10am–5.30pm and Sunday 11am–5pm; November to March: Monday to Saturday 10am–4.30pm, Sunday 2–4.30pm; tel: 01333-310 628), which is housed in a 16th–19th century complex that once served as fishermen's stores and net lofts. The museum has a number of boats and a good aquarium.

Anstruther practically coalesces with **Pittenweem** where **The Gyles**, an attractive group of restored 16th-century houses at the east end of the harbour, testifies to the fact that this was once the 12th richest town in Scotland. It is now Fife's busiest fishing port.

From Pittenweem continue eastwards on the A917, then the A915, then the A911 – a total of 17 miles (27km) – to the A92, a major road running north. At the New Inn roundabout (3 miles/5km) exit on the A912 for 3 miles (5km) to the charming village of **Falkland** clinging to the lower slopes of the Lomond Hills, and its **Palace** (April to October: Monday to Saturday 11am– 4.30pm last entry, Sunday 1.30–4.30pm last entry; tel: 01337-857 397) which dominates the main street. This was the hunting seat of the Stuart kings – a palace for recreation and sport rather than for defence and warfare. Mary Queen of Scots hunted and enjoyed falconry here. A few days before James V died at Falkland on hearing of the defeat of his forces by the English at Solway Moss he learned of the birth of Mary and said: 'it cam wi' a lass and it'll gang wi' a lass', a reference to the fact that the Stuarts mounted the throne because of marriage to Bruce's daughter. However, subsequent events proved him wrong. In 1715 Rob Roy occupied the palace and levied 'contributions' from the town.

Falkland coat of arms

The architecture of the south range of the Palace is especially fine, and it brings the French Renaissance in all its glory to Scotland.

The chapel, which is still in use, is adorned with exquisite 17th-century tapestries. In the lovely gardens, which are at their very best during the summer, is the oldest royal (ie real or, as it is called in the US, 'court') tennis court in Britain. The court is still in use and when games are not being played an audiovisual display gives an insight into this intricate game, which antedates lawn tennis by several centuries.

Avid shoppers will be detained by this Royal Burgh's antique and craft shops, while the vernacular architecture of 17th–19th century houses with their lintel and marriage stones is worth looking at. **Kind Kyttocks Kitchen** on Cross Wynd (wines and spirits available if you eat) is a great place for afternoon tea.

On leaving Falkland continue on the A912 until, after 3 miles (5km), it reaches the A91 which leads, after 8 miles (13km), to the M90 motorway and back to Edinburgh in a little over an hour.

3. The Highlands and Skye

A two-day excursion to the West Highlands and Islands, visiting en route Loch Lomond, Glencoe, Fort William, Skye, Loch Ness and (hopefully) its monster, and ending at Inverness.

– Beforehand telephone Portree in Skye and Inverness for accommodation (see pages 88–9) and book a table at the Skeabost House Hotel in Portree (March to November; tel: 01470-532 202) –

Leave the west end of Edinburgh on the A8 and join the M8 motorway for Glasgow at the Newbridge roundabout. Remain on the M8 (follow the Greenock signs) until Exit 30 is reached, 57 miles (92km) from Edinburgh. Cross the Erskine Bridge (toll) onto the north shore of the River Clyde and join the A82 which is signposted Balloch and Loch Lomond. Ignoring Balloch continue northwards on the A82 which keeps to the west of the 'bonnie, bonnie' banks of Loch Lomond, the largest body of inland water in Britain. Soon the luxurious **Cameron House Hotel**, a good place to stop for coffee, is reached. Refreshed, continue on the A82 keeping your eyes peeled for, on the left, the **Thistle Bagpipe Works** where you might wish to stop.

A few miles beyond is the turning to the tiny hamlet of **Luss** which many claim to be the most beautiful village in Scotland. From the car park stroll through the village to the pier and admire 3,192-ft (973-m) high **Ben Lomond** to the north on the far side of the loch. A short motor boat trip from the pier can provide a welcome break.

Into the Highlands

Glencoe piper

Continue to Tarbet after which the loch quickly narrows and thrusts into the mountains of the Highlands before ending at Ardlui. The road continues north, climbing all the time through attractive wooded Glen Falloch with the Falls of Falloch on the right and reaches **Crianlarich**, an important road junction 81 miles (50km) from Edinburgh. Turn left through pleasant mountain and woodland scenery on the A85 for 5 miles (8km) to **Tyndrum**. Here the road to the left goes to Oban but your route is the right fork for Fort William. As the road climbs into the mountains it gradually levels off and touches the west edge of **Rannoch Moor** above Loch Tulla. This bleak and inhospitable moor is virtually unspoilt and has a haunting beauty all of its own. Scottish bog at its best – or worst in the rain.

The road continues straight and flat across the edge of the moor making for, on the left, the striking Buachaille Etive Mor, a sentinel mountain guarding the entrance to dramatic **Glencoe** and a magnet for experienced rock climbers. The road now drops down into the glen which is notorious for the dreadful massacre of 1692 when a government force, mainly Campbells, abused the hospitality of their hosts, the MacDonalds, by rising before dawn and killing many of them on the king's orders. On the left are the **Three Sisters**, a trio of threatening buttresses, and to the right is the jagged **Aonach Eagach ridge**. Beyond this, a notice just before the Glencoe Inn marks where the massacre occurred. The story is recounted at the **Visitor Centre** (April to October daily 10am–5pm; tel: 01855-811 307) which also has information on the glen's wildlife.

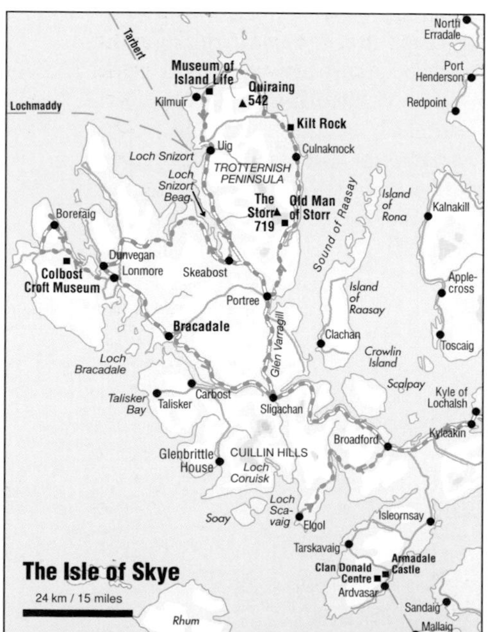

At the end of Glencoe turn right to cross the bridge and drive through Onich to reach Loch Linnhe. Nine miles (14km) north on the A82 is **Fort William** where you might wish to shop, to hear bagpipes or to eat seafood.

Continue north from Fort William on the A82 to **Spean Bridge** beyond which is an impressive monument to the World

War II Commandos who trained in this region. From here there are superb views of **Ben Nevis**, Britain's highest mountain (4,406ft/ 1,344m). Continue on the A82 along the shore of Loch Lochy to Invergarry crossing en route the **Caledonian Canal** at the south end of Loch Oich. The canal joins Scotland's east and west coasts and, for sailing and fishing boats, is a happy alternative to going around the stormy northern tip. It links the 38 miles (61km) of lochs Lochy, Oich and Ness which lie in the natural geological fault called the Great Glen with 22 miles (36km) of man-made cuttings and 38 locks. (Boats passing through these locks may delay your journey.) The canal, begun by Thomas Telford in the first half of the 19th century, took 44 years to complete.

At **Invergarry** turn left onto the A87 (signposted Kyle of Lochalsh – 46 miles), which quickly climbs into superb scenery and a glorious viewpoint high above lochs Garry and Loyne. After 12 miles (20km) the junction with the A887 is reached. For the next 19 miles (30km) the road makes its way through magnificent mountain and glen scenery: signs of man have almost evaporated. After hugging the north bank of Loch Cluanie, whose beauty is not marred by a hydro-electric scheme, for about 8 miles (13km), an isolated inn of that name is reached – a good place to stop for refreshment.

Much-photographed Eilean Donan Castle

The A87 now starts its descent through **Glen Shiel** which is deeply enclosed by lofty mountain ranges. The road passes the slopes of the renowned Five Sisters of Kintail rising sheer on the right, and exits from Glen Shiel at Shiel Bridge. It now turns right, around the head of Loch Duich and, after about 8 miles (13km) the fairytale castle of **Eilean Donan** comes into view. The castle – the most photographed in Scotland – sits on its own tiny island just off the shore, to which it is joined by a short causeway. Do not be too upset if you arrive outside opening hours (April to September: daily 10am–5.30pm; tel: 01599-555 202), for the glory of this completely restored castle is mainly in its exterior.

Continue for a further 7 miles (11km) to **Kyle of Lochalsh** and cross the one-mile-long bridge to enchanting Skye. Here, follow the A850 for 8 miles (13km) to **Broadford** from where, if time permits (the goal this evening is Portree, the capital of Skye, 26 miles/42km on), a detour can be made on the B8083 to **Elgol** and **Loch Scavaig**. The return trip is 28 miles (46km) on a tortu-

Over the sea to Skye

Loch Coruisk

ous road but the journey is well worthwhile with superb views of the serrated main ridge of the Cuillin Mountains and several Hebridean islands. From Elgol, again if time permits, motorboats will take you to the wild and beautiful **Loch Coruisk** where the mountains sweep straight up from the sea. (Alternatively, consider making this magical trip tomorrow morning before returning to the mainland.)

Back on the main road the A850 continues through Sligachan, a base for serious climbers, and then descends into **Portree** which is protected by the **Island of Raasay**. Johnson and Boswell dined here in the Royal Hotel (formerly MacNab's), where, a quarter of a century before, Prince Charlie bade farewell to Flora MacDonald with the words 'for all that has happened I hope, Madam, we shall meet in St James [then the Royal Palace in London] yet': they never did.

A superb, moderately-priced dinner can be enjoyed in glorious surroundings at the **Skeabost House Hotel**, 4 miles (7km) north of Portree on the A850. Fresh salmon, venison and Skye lamb are specialities. The hotel, a former hunting lodge in beautiful woodlands and gardens on the shore of Loch Snizort, also offers good accommodation. In the heart of Portree and down at the harbour is the less expensive **Rosedale Hotel** (*see page 75 for details*).

Next morning, continuing north on the A855, you will emerge onto the **Trotternish Peninsula** with beautiful rock scenery and breathtaking views. Soon the 2,360ft (719m) Storr, shaped like a crown, is passed. To its east stands the **Old Man of Storr**, an isolated 150-ft (45-m) pinnacle of rock, and further north is Kilt Rock, a sea cliff with a fanciful relationship to a kilt. A further 2 miles (4km) leads to Staffin immediately beyond which stands the **Quiraing**, so broken up with massive rock faces that it looks like a mountain range in miniature.

A Celtic cross in **Kilmuir** churchyard just beyond the tip of the peninsula (24 miles/39km from Portree) marks where Flora MacDonald lies buried, wrapped in a sheet from the bed in which the fugitive prince had slept. If the day is clear and you look west you can enjoy magnificent views of the Outer Hebrides from where Charlie and Flora had fled to Skye. Close to the churchyard is the **Skye Museum of Island Life** (April to October:

Dunvegan Castle

The Quiraing

Monday to Saturday 9am–5.30pm; tel: 01470-552 206) where seven thatched cottages demonstrate how crofters lived.

Travel south on the west side of the peninsula and you will soon reach **Uig**, an attractive fishing port where white-painted houses are set in green fields which sweep up from the bay flanked by high cliffs. The A855 now becomes the A856 and after 11 miles (18km) at the junction with the A850 which continues westwards for 19 miles (31km) to **Dunvegan Castle** (summer: daily 10am–5.30pm; winter: 11am–4pm; tel: 01470-521 206) which has been home to the MacLeods of Skye for the past 700 years. No other Scottish castle has a record of such continuous occupation.

The stuccoed exterior may lack the splendour of many other castles but the interior is another matter, with a wealth of paintings and memorabilia including a painting of Dr Johnson by Joshua Reynolds and a lock of Bonnie Prince Charlie's hair. Best known of the castle's treasure is the 'Faiery Flag', a torn, faded fragment of yellow silk spotted with red which is endowed with magical properties which will be exhausted once it has been used three times. So far it has twice been invoked. Also on view is the 4-pint horn of 'Rory Mor' which is filled with claret and drunk by each new chieftain 'without falling down or setting down'. Bonnie boat trips, with great sightings of seals, can be made from the castle's jetty.

If you have not lingered too long over coffee at the Castle's tearoom then a couple of miles south down the A863 turn right at **Lonmore** and drive along the B884 for 12 miles (20km), stopping en route at the **Colbost Croft Museum** (Easter to October: daily 9.30am–6pm; tel: 01470-521 296), at Glendale for the **Holmisdale House Toy Museum** (Monday to Saturday 10am–6pm; tel: 01470-511 240) and at **Boreraig**, as much a shrine to bagpipe music lovers as Salzburg is to lovers of Mozart. The **MacCrimmon Piping Centre** here (Tuesday to Saturday 11am–5.30pm; tel: 01470-511 316) is a tribute to the MacCrimmon family who for 300 years were hereditary pipers to the MacLeods.

Back to the A863 Sligachan road which follows the shores of Loch Bracadale, one of the most magnificent fjords of the west coast with the black basalt wall of Talisker Head beckoning. At **Dun Beag**, near Bracadale, stop to look at the well-preserved *broch*, a circular Iron Age fortified building. After 24 miles (38km) on the A863 Sligachan is reached and the A850 rejoined for the return trip to Kyleakin and the ferry.

Feeling sad at leaving Skye? Then prolong your visit for a wee while by stopping for lunch at the **Lochalsh Hotel** from where there are glorious views of the 'misty island'. Leave Kyle of Lochalsh by the A87 and, after 5 miles (8km), turn left onto the A890 which climbs steeply through South Strome Forest to arrive, after another 5 miles, above Stromeferry, where a narrow neck separates the inner and outer portions of Loch Carron. Many years have passed since a ferry operated here. Glorious vistas, including the Cuillins, can be savoured from a viewpoint. The road now descends and it is a magnificent 6-mile (4-km) run along the shore of Loch Carron to Strathcarron where you turn right along the A890 signposted Achnasheen.

The Red Cuillins

The road now follows the River Carron with the deer-haunted Achnashellach Forest thick with spruce, willow, birch, oak and holly on the right and past lochs Gowan and Scaven and after 18 miles (29km) arrives at the bleakly sited and scattered hamlet of **Achnasheen**. When Queen Victoria arrived here one day last century the Presbyterian landlord of the station's hotel refused to give Her Majesty fresh horses and would not post her mail: it was Sunday.

Turn right onto the A832 which crosses open moorland and passes Loch Luichart and after 17 miles (28km) arrives at Garve. The region again becomes wooded until Contin (7 miles/11km) is reached. A short detour of 2 miles (3km) to the left of the main road ends at elegant **Strathpeffer** which still emanates the distinguished atmosphere of the Victorian spa town that it once was. You can taste the waters (horrible) in the new Pump Room. Rich agricultural land has now replaced forest and moor as the road continues to a roundabout at **Muir of Ord**. If you have not yet visited a distillery then you have your chance at the **Glen Ord Distillery** (March to October: Monday to Friday 9.30am–5pm; July and September: also Saturday 9.30am–5pm and Sunday 12.30–5pm; restricted hours in winter; tel: 01463-872 004).

Follow for 14 miles (23km) the sign to the small town of **Beauly** whose spacious square is more continental than Scottish. The **Priory Hotel** is an excellent place to stop for a scrumptious afternoon tea. Next door is **Campbell and Company**, a traditional family haberdasher, with a superb selection of tweeds, woollens, tartans and the like. Orders for custom-made clothing are taken. From Beauly continue on the A9 but rather than proceeding directly to Inverness turn right after 4 miles (6km) onto the A833 which runs due south through lovely Glen Convinth for 14 miles (23km) to join the A831. A left turn and you are immediately in the busy village of

Distillery towers

Drumnadrochit and on the A82 which runs along Loch Ness.

Turn right (south) for 2 miles (4km) to reach the parking lot of **Urquhart Castle**, once one of Scotland's largest castles, which is spread over a high grassy knoll overlooking the loch and from where most sightings of Nessie (the Loch Ness Monster) have been made. If you feel energetic make the short, steep descent from the parking lot to the castle (April to September daily 9.30am–5.45pm last entry; extended hours in July and August; rest of year: 9.30am–3.45pm last entry; tel: 01456-450 551). After this, back to Drumnadrochit to visit the **Original Loch Ness Visitor Centre** (daily 9am–5pm, till 9pm in July and August; tel: 01456-450 342) at the Loch Ness Lodge Hotel, a comprehensive and fascinating place. Immediately beyond this is the **Official Loch Ness Monster Exhibition** at the Drumnadrochit Hotel, a multimedia history of the loch and its ecology. The hotel offers boat trips on the loch (daily; hours vary according to season; tel: 01456-450 573).

A relaxed drive northwards along the loch's shore brings you after 14 miles (22km) to **Inverness**, the 'Capital of the Highlands'. The town mainly lies on the right bank of the river where **Inverness Castle**, a modern 19th-century affair, occupies a prominent position looking down on the River Ness. Envy the fishermen as you cross the river: surely this is one of the few locations in the world where salmon are landed within yards of the town hall. To charter a boat contact Caley Cruises (April to October, tel: 01463-236 328).

In the evening you might wish to visit and to dine modestly at the **Eden Court Theatre** (Bishops Road, tel: 01463-234 234), a handsome multi-purpose theatre.

Urquhart Castle in its superb setting on Loch Ness

Shops usually open at 9am and close at 5.30 or 6pm. On Thursday evenings some stores in Edinburgh remain open until 8pm. Several bookshops in the capital stay open until 9 or 10pm. Sunday opening with shorter hours (noon–4pm) is fairly common. Outside the cities each town has its own early (1pm) closing day.

Value Added Tax (VAT) at 17.5 percent is added to all purchases except books and food. Some large stores will deduct this at the time of sale when the goods are being shipped directly from the store to a non-EU country. In other cases, visitors should obtain a receipt which can be stamped by Customs officers who inspect the goods at ports or airports of exit; the receipt can then be sent to the store which will mail a VAT refund.

Edinburgh

Glasgow may offer more choice than Edinburgh in its big, modern shopping centres, but for the visitor the capital is ideal for shopping because of its high concentration of interesting and typical Scottish stores in the compact city centre.

The New Town

Dominating the east end of the principal shopping thoroughfare, Princes Street, is the elegant **Jenners** building. Founded in 1838, this is the oldest independent department store in Europe. Six floors burst with quality goods and a full interpreter service is at hand. Other department stores, both at the west end of Princes Street, are **House of Fraser** and **Debenhams**. This one road is also home to no less than three branches of **Marks and Spencer**, a byword in Britain for quality and value: at No. 54 (menswear, childrenswear, food, bureau de change); No. 91 (ladieswear), and No. 104 (home store).

These days Princes Street is otherwise dominated by the 'high street' fashion chains that can be found in every big town in Britain (among them Next, Oasis, C&A, BhS, Burton, Top Shop) and music retailer Virgin Megastore. However, several well-established, traditional outfitters have remained, including **Burberry's** and the **Scotch House** (Nos 39–41). The left side of the store is devoted to Burberry's English clothing and the right side to the Scotch House's Scottish clothing, and the building also houses the Scottish Tartans Museum. Further on, going westwards, are **Jaeger** (No. 87), **Viyella** (No. 119A) and **Laura Ashley** (No. 126). Good middle-of-the-road Scottish wools at modest prices are available at the **Edinburgh Woollen Mill** (Nos 62 and 139) while lovers of tartan can select from more than 650 designs at **Hector Russell Kiltmaker** (No. 95), which also offers an excellent selection of Scottish gifts.

Edinburgh is a mecca for book lovers and there is a branch of **Waterstones** at either end of the street.

Immediately beyond the east end of Princes Street stands the **St James Centre** with its anchor tenant **John Lewis**, a giant selling simply everything of excellent quality. More interesting for the tourist is the **Waverley Shopping Centre** at the eponymous railway station which is home to some 80 shops. These include **The Ringmaker**, where you can commission your own jewellery to be made up from precious metals; **Scotland in Miniature** (stall beside the food hall) which stocks at fairly modest prices about 40 different hand-painted miniatures of Scottish landmarks, including one of Edinburgh Castle. You could also visit **The Whisky Shop**, which has an enormous selection of the precious amber fluid, just in case you haven't yet found your favourite malt.

Almost as long as, and parallel to Princes Street is characterful Rose Street, a narrow, cobbled lane in which outside tables from pubs and restaurants vie with individual shops. Highlights include the best outdoor clothing and equipment retailer in Edinburgh, **Graham Tiso**, which occupies four floors at Nos 115/123, and **Get Shirty** (No. 134), which as its name suggests has a wonderful selection of shirts.

Also parallel, another block north up the hill, exciting upmarket shopping is found on a short stretch of elegant George Street, including both high-class traditional retailers and newer incumbents mostly concentrating on designer fashion. (Recently a number of trendy bars and eateries have joined them.) In the traditional category are **Hamilton and Inches** (No. 87) and **Mappin and Webb** (No. 88), two excellent if rather expensive jewellers. Mature ladies in search of exclusive outfits can visit **Escada** at No. 35a. To please both sexes, **Austin Reed** (No. 41) carries well-made traditional men's and ladies' clothing. For the younger market, fashion stores include **Jigsaw** (No. 49), **Karen Millen** (No. 53), **French Connection** (Nos 68–70) and **Cruise** (No. 94). The branch of **Laura Ashley** at No. 90 George Street is devoted to its home furnishings range.

Justerini and Brooks (No. 45) has been supplying fine wines since 1749. Their range of malts is not to be ignored, and they also carry aromatic Havana cigars and drinking accessories. **James Allen** (No. 32) is a long-established Scottish shoe company. **Phillips** and **Sotherby's** auction rooms are at Nos 65 and 112 respectively. **James Thin** (No. 57) is an Edinburgh-owned bookstore and stationer – there's also a larger branch on South Bridge Road, catering to Edinburgh University students – and another branch of Waterstones is at No. 83.

Parallel to George Street on its north side is another narrow cobbled lane, Thistle Street, where **Joseph H. Bonnar** (No. 72) boasts an outstanding collection of antique and period jewellery, **Laurance Black** (No. 60) sells Scottish antiques and **Jane Davidson** (No. 52) stocks elegant designer clothes.

If you are in the north end of the New Town but want to find an old-fashioned Highland dress retailer, make for **Stewart Christie** (63 Queen Street), founded in 1792 as a tailor and breeches and livery maker, a tradition continued to this day. From here it is a stone's throw to **John Dickson & Son** (21 Frederick Street), one of Britain's most famous gun-making companies and the largest Scottish retailer for guns (secondhand guns are also stocked), fishing tackle, sporting clothing and sporting prints. **Blacks** at No. 24 is a smaller offshoot of London's excellent outdoor shop of the same name.

The Royal Mile

Tartan, cashmere and all Scottish souvenirs are in plentiful supply on the Royal Mile in the Old Town. Immediately on

leaving the castle, you will find the **Edinburgh Old Town Weaving Company** on Castlehill, consisting of a shop selling Highland dress and other Scottish products and **Geoffrey's Tartan Weaving Mill and Exhibition**: a working mill and exhibition illustrating how tartan is woven, where you can also have a go yourself (Monday to Saturday 9am–5.30pm, Sunday 10am–5pm). For more of the traditional wares of Scotland visit nearby **Murray Brothers**, **John Morrison Highland Outfitters** and the **Edinburgh Woollen Mill**, plus further down on the High Street **Hector Russell Kiltmaker** (at Nos 137–141) and the **Celtic Craft Centre** (No. 101). Bagpipes are made and sold by **Clan Bagpipes** (13a James Court, off Lawnmarket).

Those who delight in knitwear will discover paradise on the Royal Mile. **Judith Glue**'s (64 High Street) pure new wool, Orkney-made originals have designs featuring Viking runic script. Round the corner at the foot of Victoria Street (No. 66 Grassmarket) is **Bill Baber** who uses innovative techniques and colour blending to produce superb one-off knitwear garments in soft wool and linen. Back on the Royal Mile, on the bottom stretch, colour is brilliant at **Ragamuffin** (276 Canongate), which carries a bewitching collection of highly original knitwear.

Souvenirs on the Royal Mile

Canongate Jerseys (166 Canongate) makes original knitwear designs based mainly on Celtic, Pictish and Fair Isle patterns. If cashmere is your baby then visit **Designs on Cashmere** (28 High Street), **The Cashmere Store** (2 St Giles Street, opposite the cathedral square) or **Cashmere Classics** (9 St Mary's Street, off the Royal Mile further down the hill).

Still on the Royal Mile is **Scottish Gems** (24 High Street), with a good selection of silver and gold jewellery. Outstanding whisky stores on the Mile are **Royal Mile Whiskies** (379 High Street) and **Cadenhead Whisky Shop** (172 Canongate). The former carries an enormous collection of Scotch (be warned: describing whisky is the only use of the adjective 'Scotch' as opposed to 'Scottish' which won't irritate the locals) miniatures while the latter purchases whisky by the barrel which they then bottle without any mixing, prompting the claim that they are the only store in Scotland selling real whisky. **R. Somerville** (82 Canongate) is the only store in the world devoted exclusively to the sale of playing cards and tarot cards: it has more than 2,000 different packs. The **Carson Clark Gallery** (81–183 Canongate) is Scotland's only antique map specialist.

Around Town

If you have time to browse the shops beyond the core streets detailed above, there is plenty, still within a short bus ride, to detain you. In any case, don't miss Victoria Street (off George IV Bridge) and the Grassmarket below it, which make an interesting detour from Lawnmarket on the Royal Mile, the various quirky shops offering relief from predictable souvenir outlets. Commercial art galleries abound along Dundas Street in the upper New Town, and if you continue in that direction to Stockbridge, St Stephen Street is rich in antique shops and boutiques. Broughton Street (off the roundabout by John Lewis) offers a similar shopping experience. Antiques and some wonderful delicatessens feature on Leven Street/ Bruntsfield Place south-west of the city centre.

Bourne Fine Art
6 Dundas Street
Scottish 18th- and 19th-century paintings.

Calton Gallery
10 Royal Terrace
Fine British and European paintings.

Edinburgh Candles Shop
42 Candlemaker Row

Inhouse
28 Howe Street
A wide range of contemporary furniture and homeware from leading designers.

Kilberry Bagpipes
38 Lochrin Buildings, Gilmore Place
Pipes, accessories and recorded music.

Macsween of Edinburgh
155–159 Bruntsfield Place
Haggis specialists.

McNaughton's Bookshop
3a & 4a Haddington Place, Leith Walk
Large stock of antiquarian and second-hand books.

Mr Wood's Fossils
5 Cowgatehead, Grassmarket
Fossils and minerals collected from around Scotland and abroad.

Markets

Markets are not prominent in Edinburgh, but there are several Sunday markets for the determined bargain hunter (household goods, bric-a-brac, clothes, etc): the **New Street Market**, indoors in the Waverley Station car park (10am–2pm); **Greenside Car Boot Sale**, opposite John Lewis across Leith Street (10am–2pm); and outside the city centre near the airport, **Ingliston Market** (9.30am–3.30pm), which claims to be the largest open-air market in Europe.

Glasgow

In Glasgow's elegant city centre, it is pleasant to shop along pedestrianised Sauchihall, Buchanan and Argyle streets which form the main shopping area. The **Argyle Arcade**, created in 1827, is one of Britain's oldest covered shopping arcades.

The city centre also has a couple of attractively designed, enclosed shopping malls, **St Enoch Centre** (good for fashion) and **Princes Square**, both described in the *Day 2* itinerary, as well as the blander new **Buchanan Galleries**, which contains many of the major chain stores including John Lewis and Habitat. On the outskirts of the city the even newer **Braehead Centre,** situated on the waterfront alongside a maritime heritage centre, contains over 100 shops and has leisure facilities including an ice-rink.

Glasgow's premier department store is **Frasers** at 21-45 Buchanan Street. Worth seeking out is Byres Road in the West End which has some interesting shops selling bric-a-brac as well as fashion boutiques. In complete contrast, **The Barras** is an authentic Glaswegian general market which has eluded gentrification.

Drooko
11 St Vincent Place
Large souvenir, Glasgow memorabilia and collector's shop.

Glasgow School of Art Enterprises
167 Renfew Street
Mackintosh-style gifts and contemporary artwork.

Henderson the Jeweller
217 Sauchihall Street
Mackintosh-inspired jewellery and gifts beneath the Willow Tearoom.

John Smith & Son
57 St Vincent Street
Bookshop on six floors.

Tim Wright Antiques
147 Bath Street
Glasgow's largest antique shop.

Victorian Village
West Regent Street
A cluster of small antique shops under one roof.

Virginia Antique and Crafts Galleries
Old Tobacco Market, Virginia Street

Eating Out

Scotland has long been renowned for its produce from river and sea, from farm and moor. Fish is something of a speciality, with salmon being especially good. Kippers and Arbroath Smokies (haddock smoked over wood) are also delicious. Shellfish – lobsters, prawns, oysters, mussels – are unsurpassed and exported all over the world, while Aberdeen Angus beef and Border lamb are both renowned. Not to be ignored is a wide variety of local cheeses. Various dishes are distinctly Scottish, such as haggis – which is probably more enjoyable if you don't ask what is in it (heart, lungs and liver of a sheep, suet, oatmeal and onion).

Over the past decade culinary skills have matched the quality of the produce and today it is possible to enjoy superb meals served in the most elegant of restaurants as well as in simple, small spaces with scarcely more than half-a-dozen tables. The hours at which restaurants, especially smaller ones outside the main cities, serve meals tend to be less flexible than in many other countries. High tea, usually served from 5–7pm, is an interesting meal consisting usually of fish and chips or an egg dish followed by lashings of scones and pancakes and all accompanied by gallons of tea. On a more mundane level, there is no shortage of fast food outlets. Try the humble 'chippie' (fish and chip shop). Worth looking for is 'The Taste of Scotland' sign which about 450 restaurants are entitled to flaunt.

The list of establishments that follows is my personal selection. A rough guide to prices, per head, for a 3-course dinner excluding drinks: *Inexpensive* = under £10; *Moderate* = £10–20; *Expensive* = £20–30. Lunch is almost always a bit cheape[r] ... deed set lunch menus aimed at shop... and business people may be much che...

See also the itineraries for sugges... on where to go for good home-made s... and superior pub grub.

Edinburgh

Scottish Fare

Jackson's
209–213 High Street
Tel: 0131-225 1793
Atmospheric basement restaurant ser... imaginative dishes. Very popular ... tourists. Good value set lunch. *Expe*...

Merchants Restaurant
17 Merchant Street
Tel: 0131-225 4009
Innovative and varied Scottish and in... national cuisine in smart surroundi... Closed Sunday. *Moderate–expensive*

Stac Polly
8–10 Grindlay Street
Tel: 0131-229 5405
29–33 Dublin Street
Tel: 0131-556 2231
Superb and exciting traditional and m... ern cuisine in a very Scottish setting. C... 70 malt whiskies. *Moderate.*

Vintner's Rooms
The Vaults, 87 Giles Street, Leith
Tel: 0131-554 6767
Enjoy superb creatively-cooked fish di... (and other choices) accompanied by ... cellent moderately-priced wines in th... old wine merchants' auction rooms. Clo... Sunday. *Expensive*

Tea and cakes is a Scottish speciality

THE WITCHERY BY THE CASTLE
325 Castlehill, Royal Mile
Tel: 0131-225 5613
New-wave Scottish cuisine in two restaurants, each with unusual atmosphere. Excellent choice of wines. *Expensive*

French

BONARS
56–58 St Mary's Street
Tel: 0131-556 5888
Recently established restaurant serving excellent French/Scottish cuisine. *Expensive*

LE CAFÉ SAINT-HONORÉ
34 N.W. Thistle Street Lane
Tel: 0131-226 2211
Step into this pleasant bistro, leave Scotland behind and enter France. Good value lunch. Some imaginative dishes. Decent wine list. *Expensive*

POMPADOUR
Caledonian Hotel, Princes Street
Tel: 0131-459 9988
A restaurant for that special occasion. Classic wines, impeccable service and soothing piano music accompany French cuisine at dinner and 'Legends of the Scottish Table' for lunch, all served in an elegant and formal dining room. *Expensive*

PIERRE VICTOIRE
10 Victoria Street
Tel: 0131-225 1721
A limited menu and no frills, but excellent classic cuisine and decent, moderately priced wines. *Inexpensive*

Indian

INDIAN CAVALRY CLUB
3 Atholl Place
Tel: 0131-228 3282
Upmarket Indian eatery which successfully blends brasserie and restaurant. Good wine list at reasonable prices. *Moderate*

KALPNA
2/3 St Patrick's Square
Tel: 0131-667 9890
Gujarati and southern Indian vegetarian food is served in this non-smoking restaurant. Decent, moderately priced, wines. *Inexpensive*

International

THE ATRIUM
10 Cambridge Street
Tel: 0131-228 8882
The most stylish in town; in the Traverse Theatre foyer. Sophisticated menu; mellow ambience. *Expensive*

MARTINS
70 Rose Street North Lane
Tel: 0131-225 3106
A small, well-established restaurant hidden away. Limited but accomplished menu using superb fresh produce. Closed Sunday and Monday. *Expensive*

Italian

COSMO RISTORANTE
58A North Castle Street
Tel: 0131-226 6743
Long-established elegant restaurant with dining room and seats at bar. Excellent Italian wine list. *Expensive*

LA LANTERNA
83 Hanover Street
Tel: 0131-226 3090
Warm, friendly, family-run Italian. Inexpensive wines. *Moderate*

TINELLI
139 Easter Road
Tel: 0131-652 1932
Small, unpretentious restaurant with a limited menu of superb north Italian food. Splendid cheese selection. *Moderate*

Traditional dining

Mexican

Viva Mexico
41 Cockburn Street
Tel: 0131-226 5145
The longest established Mexican in Edinburgh; cosy and authentic. Good selection for vegetarians, great margaritas. *Moderate*

Oriental

Chinese Home Cooking
34 West Preston Street
Tel: 0131-668 4946
Straightforward Cantonese cooking in an informal atmosphere. Bring your own bottle. *Inexpensive*

Kweilin
19–21 Dundas Street
Tel: 0131-557 1875
One of the best Chinese restaurants in town. A large venue serving authentic Cantonese dishes, especially strong on seafood. Closed Monday. *Moderate–expensive*

Siam Erawan
48 Howe Street
Tel: 0131-226 3675
The city's best Thai restaurant, located in the New Town. Additional Erawan branches have opened in the city centre: **Erawan Express**, *176 Rose Street, tel: 0131-220 0059*, and **Erawan Oriental Thai Restaurant and Noodle Bar**, *14 South St Andrew Street, tel: 0131-556 4242*. *Moderate*

Seafood

Café Royal Oyster Bar
17a West Register Street
Tel: 0131-556 4124
An Edinburgh institution, with other branches around the city. Victorian baroque restaurant with limited seating at bar serves simple fresh seafood and steaks. *Expensive*

Creelers Seafood Bistro & Restaurant
3 Hunter Square
Tel: 0131-220 4447
Like its sister establishment on the Isle of Arran, this place specialises in imaginative cooking of fresh seafood, plus game and vegetarian dishes. *Moderate–expensive*

Vegetarian

Bann's Vegetarian Café
5 Hunter Square
Tel: 0131-226 1112
Just off the Royal Mile, with outdoor tables. Varied menu; popular and informal. *Inexpensive*

Henderson's Salad Table
94 Hanover Street
Tel: 0131-225 2131
Busy self-serve eatery in basement; real ale. Live music. *Inexpensive*

Glasgow

Ashoka Tandoori
108 Elderslie Street
Tel: 0141-221 1761
Glasgow's best Indian food. *Moderate*

Café Gondolfi
64 Albion Street
Tel: 0141-552 6813
The grandfather of modern Glasgow cafés: a blend of traditional tearoom and European-style café-restaurant. Varied, tasty dishes and half a dozen inexpensive wines available by the bottle or glass. Busy at lunchtime. *Inexpensive*

Drum and Monkey
93–95 St Vincent Street
Tel: 0141-221 6636
This is a fun bistro-like place plus small, more formal restaurant. Occupies a former bank. Limited wine list. *Moderate*

Puppet Theatre Restaurant
11 Ruthven Lane, off Byres Road
Tel: 0141-339 8444
Four small rooms, each with a different mood, in which great contemporary Scot-

tish dishes are served. Closed Monday. *Expensive*

Ristorante Caprese
217 Buchanan Street
Tel: 0141-332 3070
Caprese is a small, cheerful, well-established restaurant which offers good standard Neapolitan cooking. Family run. *Moderate*

Rogano
11 Exchange Place
Tel: 0141-248 4055
An Art Deco institution concentrating on fish. Oyster bar and bistro downstairs for less formal, lighter eating. *Expensive*

Ubiquitous Chip
12 Ashton Lane
Tel: 0141-334 5007
Long established West End restaurant serving fine traditional and modern Scottish cuisine. Excellent wine list and over 150 malt whiskies. Light meals served all day in upstairs brasserie. *Moderate–expensive*

Skye

Lochbay Seafood Restaurant
Stein, Waternish
Tel: 01470-592 235
An informal restaurant with an owner who firmly believes that if the fish is truly fresh it is diminished by an elaborate sauce. The freshest examples of shark and skate you are likely to taste. Also serves common shellfish and wild salmon. *Moderate*

Rosedale Hotel
Beaumont Crescent, Portree
Tel: 01478-613 131
Taste of Scotland member charmingly situated on the waterfront. *Moderate*

Skeabost House Hotel
A850, by Portree
Tel: 01470-532 202
See Excursion 3, page 64. Expensive.

Three Chimneys Restaurant
Colbost, by Dunvegan
Tel: 01470-511 258
Seafood platter and lobster feast – all of which is of course caught locally – plus scrumptious desserts are specialities at candelit dinner in this former croft. Seating is very limited, so book ahead. No smoking. *Moderate*

Inverness

Café One
75 Castle Street
Tel: 01463-226 200
Ultra-fresh seafood and good wines, some served by the glass. Closed Sunday. *Moderate*

Culloden House Hotel
Culloden, near Inverness
Tel: 01463-790 461
Dine in the exquisite Adam Room on local produce French-style in this architectural gem which is 3 miles (5km) south of town. *Expensive*

Glen Mhor Hotel
Glen Mhor Hotel, 9–12 Ness Bank
Tel: 01463-234 308
Pleasant Scottish restaurant overlooking river which serves imaginatively cooked local produce. Also a Scottish/ethnic bistro. *Expensive*

Try the shellfish

Although Scotland doesn't have a strong reputation for vibrant nightlife the two main cities now cater well for the night owl, with a large number of late bars and dance clubs that stay open until 3 or 4 in the morning. High culture is offered by the Scottish National Orchestra, the Scottish Symphony Orchestra, Scottish Opera and Scottish Ballet, which all give regular concerts in both Edinburgh and Glasgow.

Theatre flourishes, with Edinburgh's Traverse Theatre and Glasgow's Citizens Theatre being two internationally renowned repertory companies. Inverness also has first-class repertory, and in summer the Pitlochry Festival Theatre gives professional performances. Commercial theatre is also alive and kicking in the major cities – major venues are the Royal Lyceum and the King's in Edinburgh and the King's in Glasgow. Even if you aren't seeing a performance, visiting the lively bar-restaurants in the Traverse in Edinburgh and the Citizens and Tron in Glasgow can be enjoyable.

In the Highlands and Islands, especially in the more isolated villages, you will come upon the occasional *ceilidh* (pronounced 'cayley'), an informal social gathering with folk music, singing and dancing. Visitors are very welcome at these lively evenings. Regular and more commercial *ceilidhs* which present the popular tourist image of a Scottish night out are regularly put on in some hotels in the cities.

Theatres

In Edinburgh

FESTIVAL THEATRE
13–29 Nicolson Street
Tel: 0131-529 6000
Opera, ballet, drama, variety and dance.

KING'S THEATRE
2 Leven Street
Tel: 0131-220 4349
Edwardian theatre with varied programme including drama, musicals, dance and pantomime.

ROYAL LYCEUM
30B Grindlay Street
Tel: 0131-229 9697
Victorian theatre offering various mainstream productions.

TRAVERSE THEATRE
10 Cambridge Street
Tel: 0131-228 1404
Fabulous state of the art building used for original new theatre.

In Glasgow

CITIZENS THEATRE
119 Gorbals Street
Tel: 0141-429 0022
Main theatre and studios show British and European classics.

KING'S THEATRE
297 Bath Street

Tel: 0141-227 5511
The leading commercial theatre.

TRON THEATRE
63 Trongate
Tel: 0141-552 4267
Stylish venue; innovative mixed programme.

Other Locations

PITLOCHRY FESTIVAL THEATRE
Pitlochry
Tel: 01796-472 680

EDEN COURT THEATRE
Bishops Road, Inverness
Tel: 01463-221 718

Ceilidhs and 'Scottish Evenings'

In Edinburgh

An evening of Scottish-style entertainment, with folk and bagpipe music, singing and dancing, with dinner included, is offered at the following venues. You are advised to book ahead.

CARLTON HIGHLAND HOTEL
North Bridge
Tel: 0131-556 7277
'Hail Caledonia', May to September, nightly at 7pm.

KING JAMES THISTLE HOTEL
St James Centre
Tel: 0131-556 0111
'Jamie's Scottish Evening', mid-April to mid-October, nightly at 7pm.

GEORGE INTERCONTINENTAL HOTEL
19–21 George Street
Tel: 0131-225 1251
May to September, Sunday to Thursday at 7pm.

In Glasgow

THE RIVERSIDE
Fox Street, off Clyde Street
Tel: 0141-248 3144
Ceilidhs Friday and Saturday from 8pm.

Other Locations

CUMMING HOTEL
Church Street, Inverness
Tel: 01463-232 531
'Scottish Showtime', June to September, Monday to Thursday at 8.30pm.

Pubs

In Edinburgh

Edinburgh has 700 pubs, the most per capita, so it is said, of any British city. Traditional opening hours are 11am–11pm, but as Scotland has less strict licensing hours than its neighbour to the south, many open until 1am. Locals will be happy to give you inside information on where to go next so you can drink right around the clock. The pubs on Rose Street are detailed in *Pick & Mix Option 3, page 43*. Other pubs are listed below, many of historical interest and furnished with stained glass and mahogany.

BEEHIVE INN
18/20 Grassmarket
Tel: 0131-225 7171
Historic features. Has a choice of nearly 400 different wines and a good restaurant.

BENNETS BAR
8 Leven Street
Tel: 0131-229 5143
Edwardian bar with leather seats. Offers its own brand of whisky and serves splendid lunches.

KAY'S BAR
39 Jamaica Street

Innovative productions are staged here

Tel: 0131-225 1858
A smoky coal fire, newspapers and classical music make this a New Town haven.

SHEEP'S HEID INN
43–45 The Causeway, Duddingston Village
Tel: 0131-656 6951
An 18th-century coaching inn whose licence dates from the 15th century complete with skittle alley. Outside barbecues in good weather.

VOLUNTEER ARMS
237 Morningside Road
Tel: 0131-447 1484
You'll become so absorbed with the memorabilia you'll forget your tipple and the sawdust on the floor. The ticking of a superb collection of antique clocks accompanies the glug glug of drinkers in this treasure trove of collectors' pieces.

YE OLDE GOLF TAVERN
30–31 Wrights Houses off Bruntsfield Place (south of Tollcross)
Tel: 0131-229 1093
The oldest pub in Edinburgh (first opened in 1456) with a spacious, comfy lounge overlooking the golf course. Menu with wholefood and vegetarian dishes and gantry with 50 malts.

Many Edinburgh pubs host live music, especially Celtic folk. They include:

BANNERMAN'S
212 Cowgate
Tel: 0131-556 3254
Basic but atmospheric, studenty pub; live rock/indie music featuring local bands on Wednesday; DJs Friday and Saturday.

MALT SHOVEL
11–15 Cockburn Street
Tel: 0131-225 6843
Dimly lit comfortable pub with vast array of whiskies: lunches, suppers. Regular live music – jazz on Tuesday.

THE ROYAL OAK
1 Infirmary Street
Tel: 0131-557 2976
Informal folk and Scottish traditional sessions every evening and Sunday lunchtimes.

RYRIE'S BAR
1 Haymarket Terrace
Tel: 0131-337 7582
Traditional Victorian pub with regular live music – blues on Thursday and Sunday.

TRON CEILIDH HOUSE
9 Hunter Square
Tel: 0131-226 0931
No longer *the* venue for jazz and folk, but still has acoustic nights on Tuesday in the cellar bar and blues one Monday a month.

In Glasgow

BABBITY BOWSTER
16 Blackfriars Street
Tel: 0141-552 5055
An 18th-century hotel pub just off the High Street, offering real ale, typical Scottish food and occasional live music.

THE HORSESHOE
17 Drury Street
Tel: 0141-229 5711
Classic Glasgow pub which claims to have the longest bar in the world. Good range of beers and good value food.

VICTORIA BAR
157 Bridgegate
Tel: 0141-552 4524
Authentic old pub, located in one of Glasgow's oldest streets by the river. Celtic folk Friday and Saturday.

Nightclubs

Consult *The List* fortnightly events magazine for details of club nights and live music (the latter at The Venue, La Belle Angele and The Liquid Room below) in Edinburgh and Glasgow. Clubs typically open around 11pm–3am.

In Edinburgh

THE ARK
3 Semple Street
Tel: 0131-229 7733

THE CAVENDISH
3 West Tolcross
Tel: 0131-228 3252

CLUB MERCADO
36–39 Market Street
Tel: 0131-226 4224

LA BELLE ANGELE
11 Hasties Close
(off Guthrie Street)
Tel: 0131-225 7536

LEGENDS
71 Cowgate
Tel: 0131-225 8382

THE LIQUID ROOM
9c Victoria Street
Tel: 0131-225 2564

THE VENUE
17–23 Calton Roaad
Tel: 0131-557 3073

In Glasgow

ARCHAOS
25 Queen Street
Tel: 0141-204 3189

THE TUNNEL
84 Mitchell Street
Tel: 0141-204 1000

VICTORIA'S
98 Sauchiehall Street, Glasgow
Tel: 0141-332 1444

Gay Scene

In Edinburgh

BLUE MOON CAFÉ
36 Broughton Street
Tel: 0131-557 0911

CAFÉ KUDOS
22 Greenside Place
Tel: 0131-558 1270

In Glasgow

CAFE DEL MONICA'S
68 Virginia Street
Tel: 0141-552 4803

Casinos

Gambling houses are not allowed to advertise in the UK and an archaic law requires you to become a member of a casino 48 hours before you play. Membership is free. Men must wear a jacket and tie.

Edinburgh

LADBROKES MAYBURY CASINO
5 South Maybury Road
Tel: 0131-338 4444

STANLEY BERKELEY CASINO CLUB
2 Rutland Place
Tel: 0131-228 4446

Many bars have live music

STANLEY CASINO MARTELL
7–11 Newington Road
Tel: 0131-667 7763

STANLEY EDINBURGH CASINO CLUB
York Place
Tel: 0131-624 2121

Glasgow

LADBROKES CHEVALIER CASINO
95 Hope Street
Tel: 0141-226 3856

LADBROKES PRINCES CASINO
528 Sauchiehall Street
Tel: 0141-332 8171

STANLEY BERKELEY CASINO CLUB
Berkeley Street
Tel: 0141-332 0992

Calendar of Special Events

Highland Gatherings or Games and, to a lesser extent, Border Ridings are held throughout the summer. Gatherings are usually on Saturday or Sunday, occasionally midweek. Most renowned is Braemar which is listed below with some other major gatherings. Contact the local tourist office to confirm dates.

Riding festivals are held in Border towns in early summer, recalling the Middle Ages when ride-outs defined and controlled border boundaries.

JANUARY

Burns Night (25th): throughout the country the poet's birthday is celebrated with traditional dinners.

Celtic Connections (late Jan–early Feb, Glasgow): two weeks of Celtic music, art and culture.

APRIL

Edinburgh Science Festival (mid-month): lots of fascinating displays and talks, especially good for children.

MAY

Scottish International Children's Festival (3rd or last week), Edinburgh: the biggest performing arts event for young people in Scotland.

Highland Festival (late May–early June, various venues): large variety of events across the region celebrating Highland culture.

Pitlochry Festival Theatre (until October): up to eight plays in repertory each week plus other events.

JUNE

Hawick Common Riding (1st Friday, Saturday): see introductory text for explanation.

Glenmorangie Camanachd Shinty Cup Final (1st Saturday; location varies): enjoy legalised mayhem when watching 'Scotland's ain game'.

Selkirk Common Riding (2nd week): culminates in a moving casting of the colours ceremony.

St Magnus Festival (3rd or 4th week) Orkney: a six-day event with music, drama, poetry and visual arts.

Royal Highland Show (3rd week): *the* Agricultural Show; held at Ingliston showground, about 7 miles (11km) from Edinburgh.

The Braemar Games

A feature of every Highland Games

JULY

International Jazz Festival (early July), Glasgow: Britain's most comprehensive jazz event.
Balloch (Loch Lomond) Highland Games (3rd Saturday): World Championship for Heavy Events.
Loch Lomond World Invitational Golf Championship (2nd week); Luss.
British Open Golf Championship (3rd week): *the* Open is often held on one of the Scottish courses – Turnberry, St Andrews, Muirfield, Troon, Carnoustie.
Edinburgh International Jazz and Blues Festival (late July/early August).

AUGUST

World Pipe Band Championships (3rd Saturday), Glasgow: pipers from throughout the world blow their lungs out. Highland Games held at same venue at same time.
Cowal Highland Gathering (3rd Saturday), Dunoon: well-established games held in attractive surroundings.
Edinburgh International Film Festival (lasts 2 weeks): one of the major film festivals in the world.
Edinburgh International Festival (mid-August to the start of September): the 'daddy' of all cultural festivals, with concerts, opera, dance and theatre.
Edinburgh Military Tattoo (first 3 weeks): castle esplanade.
Edinburgh Fringe (2nd–4th weeks): grew up as a festival within a festival, now by far the biggest event in Edinburgh's festival season. Specialises in off-beat and *avant-garde* entertainment including comedy and street theatre.
Lammas Fair and Market (2nd weekend), St Andrews: one of Scotland's oldest street fairs.
Edinburgh International Book Festival (3rd and 4th weeks): the world's biggest public celebration of books, featuring major authors.

SEPTEMBER

Braemar Highland Gathering (1st Saturday): invariably attended by royalty who spend the summer at their nearby castle at Balmoral.
Blairgowrie Highland Games (1st Sunday): 'society' attends this gathering in force.

OCTOBER

The National Mod (2nd week; venue changes annually): traditional Scottish culture – singing, fiddle playing, clarsach playing, bagpipes and poetry.

DECEMBER

Edinburgh Hogmanay (30th December–2nd January): Immensely popular four-day shindig with balls, fun-fair, fire processions, fireworks, etc. Tickets (free) need to be booked in advance for access to the city centre.
Hogmanay (31st): lively celebrations everywhere in Scotland. Some traditions have faded but processions involving fire are still held in Biggar, Comrie and Stonehaven.

Fringe Festival performers

Practical Information

GETTING THERE

By Air

Scotland is reasonably well served by direct non-stop flights from North America and from parts of Europe. British Airways and Continental Airlines fly from New York to Glasgow; American Airlines flies from Chicago to Glasgow in summer; and Air Canada from Toronto to Glasgow. In addition, Icelandair flies from Reykjavik and Aer Lingus from Dublin to both Edinburgh and Glasgow.

Air France has flights from Paris to Edinburgh; KLM Air UK has flights from Amsterdam to both Edinburgh and Glasgow; Sabena flies from Brussels to Edinburgh and Glasgow; and British Midland flies from Copenhagen to Edinburgh.

Your carriage awaits

There are excellent services from London (Heathrow, Gatwick, London City, Luton and Stansted airports) and several English regional airports to Edinburgh and Glasgow, plus more limited services to Aberdeen and Inverness. Airlines flying these routes include British Airways, Go (a British Airways cut-price subsidiary), British Midland, KLM Air UK, Ryanair and EasyJet, which was the first company to offer no-frills flights with very reasonably-priced fares. (Cheap fares are subject to limited availability, so book early.) Flights from London to either Edinburgh or Glasgow will take about 70 minutes; flights from London to Aberdeen or Inverness will take about 100 minutes.

Edinburgh airport (tel: 0131-333 1000) is 6 miles (10km) west of the city centre, and there are good roads and a useful air-link bus service into the heart of town.

Glasgow international airport (tel: 0141-887 1111) is 8 miles (13km) west of the city centre. A coach service runs between the airport and Anderston and Buchanan Street bus stations, both of which are in the heart of the city.

By Rail

There are frequent InterCity rail services to Scotland from many mainline railway stations in England. It takes about 4 hours from London (Kings Cross) to Edinburgh, and about 5½ hours from London (Euston or Kings Cross) to Glasgow. Sleeper and Motorail services run between London (Euston) and Edinburgh, Glasgow, Aberdeen, Inverness and Fort William.

A limited number of cheap (APEX) fares are available for those booking at least 7 days in advance of travelling. Try to avoid travelling on Sundays when services are often curtailed due to engineering works. For rail-travel information call the centralised number, 0345-484 950.

Ferries connect the islands

By Road

Good motorway connections link Scotland to England and Wales. The M1/M6 is the quickest route, though heavily congested at the southern end. The A1, a more easterly approach, is longer but may be a better bet if you plan to make one or two stopovers (*eg* York) on the way. Edinburgh and Glasgow are about 400 miles (643km) from London.

By Bus

Scottish Citylink (tel: 0990-505 050) and National Express (tel: 0990-808 080) operate daytime and overnight coaches from England to Scotland. The journey takes about 8 hours from London to Edinburgh or Glasgow. They are not as comfortable or fast as trains, but less expensive unless you buy an APEX fare (see *By Rail*).

TRAVEL ESSENTIALS

Visas

Americans, Canadians, citizens of EC countries and most Commonwealth countries do not require visas to enter Scotland.

Weather

No matter what you say about Scottish weather you are bound to be wrong. Nowhere can it be depended upon: wait a moment and it will change. Summer is, in Scotland, a somewhat misleading expression yet there are, albeit rare, occasions when the mercury soars to 80 degrees Fahrenheit (over 26°C). In winter, when night-time temperatures can be well below freezing, snow often falls on high ground and not infrequently at lower levels too. For what it is worth, April, May and June are usually drier than July, August and September and the west is generally wetter and warmer than the east – noticeably warmer in the winter months. For weather forecasts telephone 0891-500 422 (Edinburgh, South Fife, Lothian and Borders); 0891-500 421 (Glasgow, Clyde Coast, Argyll)); 0891-500 423 (Tayside, Central, East Fife); 0891-500 424 (Grampians and East Highlands); 0891-500 425 (Northwest Scotland).

What to Wear

Given the weather one should never be without an umbrella, raincoat and warm sweater. Neither in summer should you be without light clothes. A few restaurants do demand 'jacket and tie'.

Electricity

220 volts is standard. Hotels usually have dual 220/110-volt sockets for razors. If you are visiting from abroad you will probably need an adaptor to link other small electrical appliances to the three-pin sockets universal in Britain; it is usually easier to find these at home before leaving for Scotland.

Time

Greenwich Mean Time (GMT) is in operation from mid-October to late March when the clocks move forward one hour and British Summer Time operates.

Holidays

Local, public and bank holidays can be frustrating for visitors but usually there will be a small shop open somewhere on public holidays which are 25 and 26 December, 1 and 2 January and Good Friday. Other national holidays: May Day (first Monday in May), Spring Bank Holiday (last Monday in May), Summer Bank Holiday (first Monday in August).

MONEY MATTERS

Visitors are allowed to bring in as much currency and as many travellers' cheques as they wish.

Banks

Scotland has its own banks – the Royal Bank of Scotland, the Bank of Scotland

and the Clydesdale. They issue their own bank notes which circulate alongside Bank of England notes. Don't expect consistent opening hours but most banks are open Monday–Friday 9.30am–4pm with an extension to 5.30pm on Thursday.

Currency

The British pound is divided into 100 pence. The coins used are 1p, 2p, 5p, 10p, 20p, 50p and £1. In Scotland the £1 coin is not nearly so common as in England and £1 notes still circulate along with notes in demoninations of £5, £10, £20, £50 and £100. Technically Scottish bank notes are not legal tender in England and Wales. However, most shops accept them and English banks will readily change them for you.

Travellers' Cheques

Eurocheques and Eurocard can be used at banks and travellers' cheques can be cashed at banks, bureaux de change and many hotels.

Credit Cards

MasterCard and Visa are the most commonly acceptable credit cards, followed by American Express and Diners Club. Small guest houses, bed-and-breakfast places and some restaurants require payment in cash.

Tipping

Tipping is voluntary but waiters, taxi-drivers and hairdressers expect 10–15 percent of the bill, up to 20 percent for above-average service. Railway porters expect about £1.

GETTING AROUND

Travel by Car

Visitors can drive on a valid foreign licence for a maximum of 12 months. Driving is on the left. Speed limits are as indicated or, if not indicated, 70mph (110kph) on motorways and dual carriageways, 60mph (95kph) on other roads and 30mph (50kph) in built-up areas. A single yellow line at the kerbside indicates no daytime parking: a double yellow line indicates no parking at any time. Zig-zags near pedestrian crossings also indicate no parking at any time. Drivers and passengers must wear seatbelts by law.

Single lane roads are common in the countryside but have passing places. Drivers are almost invariably extremely courteous in these situations. Petrol – unleaded available – is sold by the litre (4½ litres = 1⅕ American gallons).

Membership of a recognised automobile club in your own country allows the visitor certain facilities in British automobile clubs. The Royal Automobile Club (RAC) is at 200 Finnieston Street, Glasgow, G3 8NZ (tel: 0141-248 4444), but call 0800-828282 if you break down. The Automobile Association (AA) operates a telephone enquiries service on 0990-500 600, but call 0800-887 766 if you break down. Both offer literature, roadside assistance and recovery services. The AA is member-oriented while the RAC is happy to assist foreign visitors.

Car Hire

Self-drive rental costs £20 upwards, depending on the company, type of car and duration of rental. Rates fall in the off season – October to April.

Companies in Edinburgh include: *Arnold Clark*, Lochrin Place, tel: 0131-228 4747; *Avis Rent-a-Car*, 100 Dalry Road, tel: 0131-337 6363; *Budget Rent-a-Car*, 111 Glasgow Road, tel: 0845-606 6669; *Europcar UK Ltd*, 24 East London Street, Tel: 0131-557 3456; *Hertz Rent-a-Car*, 10 Picardy Place, tel: 0131-556 8311; *Mitchells Self Drive*, 32 Torphichen Street, tel: 0131-229 5384.

At Edinburgh airport are: *Avis*, tel: 0131-333 5100; *Europcar*, tel: 0131-333 2588 and *Hertz*, tel: 0131-333 1019.

Exhilarating driving

Companies in Glasgow include: *Arnold Clark*, Castlebank Street, tel: 0141-839 9886; *Avis Rent-a-Car*, 161 North Street, tel: 0141-221 2827; *Budget Rent-a-Car*, 101 Waterloo Street, tel: 0845-606 6669; *Europcar UK Ltd*, 38 Anderson Quay, tel: 0141-248 8788; *Hertz Rent-a-Car*, 106 Waterloo Street, tel: 0141-248 7736; *Mitchells Self Drive*, 47 McAlpine Street, tel: 0141-221 8461.

At Glasgow airport are: *Avis*, tel: 0141-887 2261; *Budget*, Inchinnan Road, tel: 0800-626 063; *Europcar*, tel: 0141-887 0414; *Hertz*, tel: 0141-887 2451; *Mitchells Self Drive*, tel: 0141-887 7866.

Companies in Inverness include: *Budget Rent-a-Car*, Railway Terrace, tel: 01463-713 333; *Europcar UK Ltd*, Highlander Service Station, Millburn Road, tel: 01463-235 337; *Hertz Rent-a-Car*, Station Square, tel: 01463-711 479; *Arnold Clark Peugeot*, Harbour Road, tel: 01463-231 536.

Companies operating from Inverness airport include: *Avis*, tel: 01667-462 787, and *Hertz*, tel: 01667-462 652.

Taxis

Metered taxis are found in the main cities and at airports. There are extra charges after midnight and for trips beyond city boundaries. You may also be approached by unlicensed drivers who are best avoided – usually because they don't know their way. Compared to most European countries and the US taxis are not that expensive. Visitors from Asia (not Japan) and Greece will find them costly.

Limousine Service

Chauffeur Drive, 111 The Loan, Loanhead, tel: 0131-440 1192; *W. L. Sleigh Ltd*, 6 Devon Place, Edinburgh, tel: 0131-337 3171; *Little's Chauffeur Drive*, 5 St Ninian's Drive, Edinburgh, tel: 0131-334 2177.

Public Transport

This is invariably comfortable but not as frequent as one would hope. Within the cities exact change is generally required. Glasgow has a 15-stop underground with 6½ miles (10km) of track. It is known locally as the Clockwork Orange and is an excellent, inexpensive way to get around the city on a wet day.

Good InterCity rail services run between Glasgow and Edinburgh and from these cities to other major cities including Aberdeen, Inverness, Perth, Stirling and to Mallaig and Fort William. It is generally agreed that the most scenic line in Britain is between Fort William and Mallaig – or is it between Inverness and Kyle of Lochalsh? During summer some trains on these lines are hauled by steam locomotives.

Simple but effective

Major towns have their own bus services. Entry is from the front and exact change usually helps. In addition buses serve rural communities and link the various towns but these are often infrequent and slow. On the other hand, InterCity services – Edinburgh or Glasgow to Aberdeen, Inverness, Fort William, Oban – are fast, fairly punctual and comfortable.

For those wanting to do some island-hopping, be reassured that the ferries are great. The main operator is Caledonian MacBrayne, whose timetable (Ferry Terminal, Gourock, PA19 1QP, tel: 01475-650 100) is indispensable and, at first glance, incomprehensible. MacBrayne has a fleet of 30 vessels which call at 53 ports on the west coast mainland and on 23 islands. They sell island hopscotch tickets and rover tickets for a driver and one passenger giving 8 or 15 days unlimited travel on most routes. Summer booking is advisable. There is plenty of small private enterprise on the west coast. In northern Scotland, the ferry schedules to Orkney and Shetland are easier to understand than those to the Western Isles. Summer booking is essential.

ACCOMMODATION

A wide range of accommodation is available, from the big chains and privately-owned country house hotels to simple bed-and-breakfast (B&B) accommodation. Prices vary from under £15 to over £100 per person per night .

How does one select a place to stay? Scottish Tourist Board approved accommodation displays an oval sign with the Tourist Board logo. On this logo, star gradings assess quality, ranging from one star (fair and acceptable) to five stars (exceptional/world class). This applies to all types of accommodation. Symbols in brochures indicate the facilities available. Some premises may still display their grading according to an older system which both tells you the extent of the facilities (indicated by the word 'listed' for the most basic facilities to five crowns for those with the most facilities) and gives a grading for quality (Approved, Commended or Highly Commended).

Staying in B&B accommodation is not only economical but is also a flexible and potentially interesting way to see the country and to meet the natives. With luck you may find the proprietor friendly and a mine of local information with suggestions about the route to take and things to see. Most better B&B establishments serve dinner, which is usually excellent and modestly priced, on request. All rooms have *en suite* bath or shower facilities unless otherwise stated.

Except for the 5-star city hotels most prices quoted include breakfast. Approximate guides to prices per person per night in a hotel double room are: *£* = below £30; *££* = £30–50; *£££* = £50–70; *££££* = above £70.

Edinburgh

ALLISON HOUSE HOTEL (24 rooms)
15–17 Mayfield Gardens
Tel: 0131-667 8049, fax: 667 5001
Two star rating from AA and RAC. *A la carte* restaurant, parking and garden. *££*

APEX INTERNATIONAL HOTEL (168 rooms)
31–35 Grassmarket
Tel: 0131-300 3456, fax: 220 5345
In a very convenient city centre location, ideal for tourists on a budget. Rooftop restaurant, parking. *££–£££*

Balmoral Hotel doorman

BALMORAL HOTEL (189 rooms)
1 Princes Street
Tel: 0131-556 1111, fax: 557 8740
The city's premier hotel, built in 1862, re-opened in 1991 after a £23 million facelift. A full leisure complex has recently been added. Many rooms have a view of the castle. Two restaurants. *££££*

BRUNTSFIELD HOTEL (75 rooms)
69–74 Bruntsfield Place
Tel: 0131-229 1393, fax: 229 5634
Beautiful town house hotel in a nice area opposite parkland 1 mile south of the city centre. *£££–££££*

CALEDONIAN HOTEL (236 rooms)
Princes Street
Tel: 0131-459 9988, fax: 225 6632
The 'Grande Dame' of Edinburgh hotels is constantly being upgraded. Many rooms with view of the castle. *££££*

CHANNINGS (48 rooms)
South Learmonth Gardens
Tel: 0131-315 2226, fax: 332 9631
A series of splendid Edwardian houses a few minutes from the city centre. Bedrooms are individually furnished. *££££*

EDINBURGH CITY TRAVEL INN (128 rooms)
1 Morrison Link

Tel: 0131-228 9819, fax: 228 9836
A laudable bid to provide economical, comfortable, no-frills accommodation in the city centre. *££–£££*

MALMAISON HOTEL (60 rooms)
1 Tower Place, Leith
Tel: 0131-468 5000, fax: 468 5002
Stylish and luxurious modern hotel on the redeveloped waterfront. Excellent value. *£££–££££*

MARRIOTT DALMAHOY HOTEL AND COUNTRY CLUB (151 rooms)
Kirknewton
Tel: 0131-333 1845, fax: 333 1433
Grand mansion 7 miles (12km) west of the city centre, 3 miles (5km) from the airport. Leisure facilities include two championship golf courses. *££–££££*

THRUMS PRIVATE HOTEL (14 rooms)
14 Minto Street, Newington
Tel: 0131-667 5545, fax: 667 8707
Detached Georgian house with garden, 5 minutes from city centre. *££*

For the following guest houses, private hotels and B&B establishments, prices per person per night are: *£* = £15–25; *££* = £25–40; £££ = more than £40. On occasions, the distinction between B&Bs, guest houses and private hotels becomes blurred, especially when the former have *en suite* facilities and serve dinner.

ASHLYN GUEST HOUSE
(8 rooms, 5 *en suite*)
42 Inverleith Row
Tel: 0131-552 2954
Ashlyn is a listed Georgian house close to the Botanic Gardens; 5 minutes drive from city centre. *££*

GALLOWAY GUEST HOUSE
(10 rooms, 6 *en suite*)
22 Dean Park Crescent
Tel: 0131-332 3672
Located in a residential area 10 minutes walk from Princes Street. *£*

GLENALMOND GUEST HOUSE (10 rooms)
25 Mayfield Gardens
Tel/fax: 0131-668 2392
Family-run Victorian house near Holyrood Park. *£–££*

SALISBURY GUEST HOUSE
(12 rooms, 9 *en suite*)
45 Salisbury Road
Tel/fax: 0131-667 1264
Georgian listed building near Holyrood Palace and Royal Mile. *£–££*

17 ABERCROMBY PLACE (9 rooms)
Tel: 0131-557 8036, fax: 558 3453
Former home of Edinburgh architect William Playsair. Parking and great views over the Fife and Queen St Gardens. *£££*

SIBBERT HOUSE (5 rooms, 4 *en suite*)
26 Northumberland Street
Tel: 0131-556 1078, fax: 557 9445
Stay with the 'Auld alliance' (France/Scotland) in the heart of the New Town. Sumptuous breakfasts. *£–££*

Glasgow

ONE DEVONSHIRE GARDENS (27 rooms)
1 Devonshire Gardens
Tel: 0141-339 2001, fax: 337 1663
Exquisite West End hotel in residential district. Each room is different and the service is deluxe and relaxed. *££££*

TOWN HOUSE HOTEL (36 rooms)
Nelson Mandela Place
Tel: 0141-332 3320, fax: 332 9756
Grand, lavishly furnished hotel in the heart of the city. *£££*

SHERBROOKE CASTLE (25 rooms)
11 Sherbrooke Avenue
Tel: 0141-427 4227, fax: 427 5685
Baronial castle 3 miles (5km) from centre. Handy for the Burrell Collection. *££*

STAKIS GLASGOW GROSVENOR (96 rooms)
Grosvenor Terrace
Tel: 0141-339 8811, 334 0710
Hotel with striking facade near Botanic Gardens, University of Glasgow and trendy Byers Road. *££*

BOSWELL HOTEL (12 rooms)
27 Mansionhouse Road
Tel: 0141-632 9812, fax: 632 5987
Small, bustling hotel on the south side of

the city with three busy bars. Near public transport. Family suites. *£*

Good quality guest houses and B&Bs charging £ = £15–20; and ££ = £20–30:

THE TOWN HOUSE (10 rooms)
4 Hughenden Terrace
Tel: 0141-357 0862, fax: 339 9605
Elegantly refurbuished Victorian townhouse in quiet conservation area in West End. *££*

ALAMO GUEST HOUSE (7 rooms, 3 *en suite*)
46 Gray Street
Tel: 0141-339 2395
Situated on pleasant, quiet road alongside Kelvingrove Park, with magnificent view from spacious dining room. *£*

Inverness

BRAE NESS HOTEL (10 rooms)
Ness Bank
Tel: 01463-712 266, fax: 231 732
Brae Ness is a welcoming, family-run hotel set beside the River Ness. No smoking. *££*

BUNCHREW HOUSE HOTEL (11 rooms)
Bunchrew
Tel: 01463-234 917, fax: 710 620
Every inch a 17th-century Scottish baronial home yet very comfortable and laidback. Bunchrew stands in 20 acres (8 hectares) of grounds on the shores of Beauly Firth, 5 miles (8km) from city. *££–£££*

COLUMBA HOTEL (86 rooms)
Ness Walk
Tel: 01463-231 391, fax: 715 526
Refurbished hotel on banks of River Ness. Close to town. *£–££*

CULDUTHEL LODGE (12 rooms)
14 Culduthel Road
Tel/fax: 01463-240 089
A splendid 19th-century house overlooking the Moray Firth, Inverness and the Black Island. Unusual circular drawing room. No smoking. *££*

CULLODEN HOUSE HOTEL (28 rooms)
Culloden
Tel: 01463-790 461, fax: 792 181
An architectural gem 3 miles (5km) east of Inverness, associated with Bonnie Prince Charlie and the Battle of Culloden. There are magnificent public rooms, and the hotel is set in forty acres (16 hectares) of grounds. Facilities include tennis, sauna, and snooker. *££££*

DUNAIN PARK HOTEL (14 rooms)
1 mile from Inverness on the A82
Tel: 01463-230 512, fax: 224 532
Georgian country house set in 6 acres (2 hectares). Wide variety of bedrooms. Elegant public rooms. Indoor swimming pool. *££££*

GLEN MHOR HOTEL (27 rooms)
9–12 Ness Bank
Tel: 01463-234 308, fax: 713 170
In quiet residential area overlooking the River Ness. *££*

JARVIS CALEDONIAN HOTEL (106 rooms)
Church Street
Tel: 01463-235 181, fax: 711 206
Elegant hotel with all facilities in city centre. *££–£££*

STATION HOTEL (67 rooms)
18 Academy Street
Tel: 01463-231 926, fax: 710 705
Distinctive Victorian city centre hotel adjacent to railway station. *££*

WHINPARK HOTEL (10 rooms)
17 Ardross Street
Tel/fax: 01463-232 549
Victorian house situated in quiet area close to River Ness. *£*

Good quality B&Bs charging £15–28 per person per night include:

EASTER DALZIEL FARMHOUSE
(3 rooms, not *en suite*)
Dalcross, East Inverness
Tel/fax: 01667-462 213
Comfortable accommodation in the 19th-century farmhouse of a working farm, with panoramic views. Home cooking.

MRS ELIZABETH CHISHOLM (3 rooms)
43 Charles Street
Tel/fax: 01463-225 689

Family-run Victorian house situated 3 minutes from the town centre. Very reasonable rates year-round.

Mrs J Emslie (2 rooms)
7 Harris Road
Tel: 01463-237 059, fax: 242 092
Comfortable, no-smoking, friendly home with lovely garden, situated in an attractive area.

The Old Rectory (4 rooms)
9 Southside Road`
Tel: 01463-220 969
Tastefully decorated Victorian house 5 minutes walk from town centre. Parking, no smoking.

Skye

Bosville Hotel (18 rooms)
Bosville Terrace, Portree
Tel: 01478-612 846, fax: 613 434
Small central hotel. *££*

Cuillin Hills Hotel (25 rooms)
Portree
Tel: 01478-612 003, fax: 613 092
Just outside Portree with views over Portree Bay to the Cuillins. *££–£££*

Glenview Inn (5 rooms)
near Portree
Tel: 01470-562 248, fax: 562 211
Small, friendly inn in one of loveliest areas of Skye. *£–££*

Rosedale Hotel (23 rooms)
Beaumont Crescent, Portree
Tel: 01478-613 131, fax: 612 531
Comfortable hotel with character, converted from former fishermen's houses situated on the waterfront. Some bedrooms are very small and the hotel is a veritable warren. *££*

Skeabost House Hotel
A850, by Portree
Tel: 01470-532 202
Family-run hotel set amid beautifully landscaped grounds. *See Excursion 3, page 64,* for further details. *££–£££*

Good quality guest houses/B&Bs charging £18–30 per person per night are:

Craiglockhart Guest House (9 rooms, 3 *en suite*)
Beaumont Terrace, Portree
Tel: 01478-612 233
Centrally situated guesthouse overlooking the harbour.

Ptarmigan (3 rooms)
Broadford (8 miles/13km from Bridge)
Tel: 01471-822 744, fax: 822 745
Delightful accommodation offering lovely views.

HEALTH & EMERGENCIES

It is advisable to have medical insurance. Citizens of European Union countries are entitled to free medical treatment under reciprocal arrangements and similar arrangements exist with some other countries. No matter which country you are from you will receive immediate emergency treatment free of charge at a hospital casualty department.

Although Scotland isn't normally associated with mosquitoes, a persistent and aggressive breed of midge exists, especially in warm humid conditions, in parts of the west coast and calls for a tough repellent.

Crime

The country is also not normally associated with crime and, even today, in rural areas, houses are not infrequently left unlocked. Yet, Glasgow grows more violent daily and Edinburgh has a high incidence of

The right place for letters

Signs also appear in Gaelic

AIDS because of drug users. It is unlikely that tourists who take normal precautions will be involved and, in most parts of the cities and in the countryside, it is perfectly safe to stroll at night.

For emergency services such as police, ambulance, the fire service or lifeboat service dial 999.

COMMUNICATIONS

Telephone Services

Traditional red telephone boxes have largely been replaced by modern glass booths. Some are operated by coins (£1, 50p, 20p and 10p); others need phonecards which can be purchased (£1, £2, £4 or £10) from post offices and newsagents; some accept major credit cards. Useful numbers are: assistance in making UK calls 100; assistance in making international calls 155; directory enquiries (a charge is made for private lines) 192; international directory enquiries 153; emergencies – police, fire and ambulance – 999.

Direct dialling is possible to most parts of the world: First dial the international access code 00, then the country code (Australia 61, Belgium 32, France 33, Germany 49, Italy 39, Japan 81, the Netherlands 31, New Zealand 64, Spain 34, Switzerland 41, US and Canada 1.) If you are using a US credit phone card, dial the relevant company's access number: SPRINT 00 801 15; AT&T 00 801 10; MCI 00 801 11.

Media

The Scotsman, printed in Edinburgh, is the national newspaper while *The Herald*, printed in Glasgow, has good middle-market coverage and is popular in and around its native city. Most popular is the tabloid *Daily Record*, a stablemate of England's *Daily Mirror*. English dailies circulate widely in Scotland. The most popular Sunday newspaper is the *Sunday Post*, which tries to be useful as well as inoffensive. *Scotland on Sunday* is the country's only quality Sunday paper other than UK-wide publications.

Scotland is poorly served by magazines. However, the *Scottish Field* and the *Scots Magazine* are good-quality monthlies which deal with Scottish topics. *The List*, an Edinburgh-based magazine, appears every two weeks and provides lively and comprehensive coverage of events in both Edinburgh and Glasgow.

Radio and television are excellent. Radio Scotland is the main BBC Scottish radio service while national BBC and commercial stations also operate. These include Radio 1, Radio 2, Radio 3, Radio 4, Radio 5 Live, Classic FM, Virgin 1215, Atlantic 252 and BBC World Service. Local commercial stations are Forth FM, Radio Clyde (1152kHz) and Clyde FM (102.5FM). Many hotels also show satellite TV channels.

LANGUAGE

Even the English agree that the 'best' English spoken is in the northeast of Scotland, in and around Inverness. In other parts of Scotland, accents can be very heavy and not infrequently give way to patois. The Highlands and Islands are experiencing a mini-renaissance of Gaelic although all Gaelic speakers are bilingual in English.

SPECTATOR SPORTS

Opportunities to watch football (soccer) and rugby abound. Both are played throughout the year except June and July. Saturday afternoon is peak viewing time but mid-week evening games and occasional Sunday afternoon games are also played. No greater rivalry exists than that between the two major Glasgow football teams – Celtic and Rangers. The former play at Parkhead, the latter at Ibrox. Until recently contests between the two were also practically religious wars, Celtic attracting Catholic support and Rangers Protestant. Both clubs regularly accommodate over 50,000 spectators. On a rather smaller scale, the principal rivals in Edinburgh are Hearts and Hibernian. The greatest rivalry among rugby teams is found in the Borders where Hawick, Kelso and Selkirk invariably vie for honours.

Professional golf tournaments in Scotland offer an opportunity to see the world's top players struggle against the elements on the demanding links courses *(see Calendar of Events)*.

Shinty, Scotland's 'ain game', which is legalised mayhem on a hockey field, is played throughout the year especially by Highlanders, which is not to say it cannot be seen in cities. The major summer sports that will interest visitors are Highland Games *(see Calendar of Events)* with dancing and piping and the throwing of a variety of objects including the caber.

USEFUL ADDRESSES

Tourist Boards

Scottish Tourist Board, 23 Ravelston Terrace, Edinburgh EH4 3EU, tel: 0131-332 2433, fax: 343 1513. Also a London office at: 19 Cockspur Street, London SW1Y 5BL, tel: 0171-930 8661, fax: 930 1817.

Historic Scotland, Longmore House, Salisbury Place, Edinburgh EH9 1SH, tel: 0131-668 8800, fax: 668 8888.

Edinburgh and Lothians Tourist Board, 3 Princes Street, Waverley Market, Edinburgh EH2 2QP, tel: 0131-473 3800, fax: 473 3881.

Greater Glasgow and Clyde Valley Tourist Board & Convention Bureau, 11 George Square, Glasgow G2 1DY, tel: 0141-204 4480, fax: 204 4772.

For the Edinburgh Festivals

The Hub Festival Centre, Castlehill, Royal Mile, tel: 0131-473 2010. Year-round multi-festivals visitor centre with ticket centre, information service, café and shop.

Fringe Box Office, 180 High Street, tel: 0131-226 5138 (bookings); 0131-226 5257 (open all year for information).

Military Tattoo Box Office, 33–34 Market Street, tel: 0131-225 1188.

FURTHER READING

Insight Guide: Scotland (Apa Publications, 2000) A comprehensive guide to Scotland and its culture.

Insight Guide: Edinburgh (Apa Publications, 1999) Lavish photographs, in-depth essays and lots of practical information.

Insight Guide: Glasgow (Apa Publications, 1996) Another guide in Insight's flagship series; comprehensive and inspiring.

Poems by Robert Burns. Many versions.

Mary Queen of Scots by Fraser, A. Mandarin.

A Journey to the Western Isles by Dr Samuel Johnson and James Boswell's *Journal of a Tour to the Hebrides*. Two accounts of the same 18th-century trip by the great lexicographer and his biographer. Oxford University Press offers a combined volume.

Bonnie Prince Charlie by MacLean, Fitzroy. Canongate.

A Concise History of Scotland by MacLean, Fitzroy. Thames and Hudson.

Road to the Isles by Cooper, Derek. Futura.

Culloden and *The Highland Clearances* by Prebble, John. Secker & Warburg. The sad tale of crofter eviction.

A Companion to Scottish Culture by Daiches, D (ed.). Arnold.

Glasgow Observed by Berry, S and Whyte, H. John Donald Publishers.

Four Scottish Journeys by Eames, Andrew. Hodder & Stoughton.

In Search of Scotland by Morton, H.V. Methuen.

Shinty: 'legalised mayhem'

Index

E

F, G

H, I

J, K

L, M

N, O, P

Q, R